HOWDIE-SKELP

Paul Muldoon

Howdie-Skelp

FARRAR STRAUS GIROUX / NEW YORK

Farrar, Straus and Giroux
120 Broadway, New York 10271

Originally published in 2021 by Faber & Faber Limited, Great Britain
Published in the United States in 2021 by Farrar, Straus and Giroux
First American paperback edition, 2022

The Library of Congress has cataloged the hardcover edition as follows:
Names: Muldoon, Paul, author.
Title: Howdie-skelp / Paul Muldoon.
Description: First American edition. | New York : Farrar, Straus and Giroux, 2021.
Identifiers: LCCN 2021028286 | ISBN 9780374602956 (hardcover)
Subjects: LCGFT: Poetry.
Classification: LCC PR6063.U367 H69 2021 | DDC 821/.914—dc23
LC record available at https://lccn.loc.gov/2021028286

Paperback ISBN: 9780374606466

Designed by Crisis

www.fsgbooks.com
www.twitter.com/fsgbooks
www.facebook.com/fsgbooks

P1

FOR MICHAEL LONGLEY

CONTENTS

Wagtail — 3

American Standard — 4

A Ruin — 42

Shoot 'Em Up — 44

Damsons — 45

Bramleys, Not Grenadiers — 53

23 Banned Poems — 54

The Dirty Protest — 89

A Postcard from Saint Bart's — 92

Mayday — 94

Anonymous: The Vikings — 96

Clegs and Midges — 97

The Fly — 101

The Pangolin, or Vasty — 103

The Ice Fishers — 107

Binge — 108

Cow Moose, Route 125, Ripton, Vermont — 112

Chipmunk — 113

The Triumph — 114

Salonica — 140

The Banisters — 143

The Sheet — 144

Le Jongleur — 146

An Item — 149

Oscar Wilde at the Pavilion Hotel — 151

Viral — 153

A Bull — 156

Plaguey Hill — 163

Acknowledgments — 179

HOWDIE-SKELP

WAGTAIL

Sometimes, as I turn a corner in County Tyrone, a roof of PVC
or corrugated iron
will scintillate no less persuasively
than an unperturbed stretch of Lower Lough Erne

abutting the lost kingdom from which my family hails.
Primarily a thatcher, my grandfather knew mange
was a complaint to which his Clydesdales
were all too prone, yet may not have recognized dementia

as a trait of the Muldoons. Sometimes a phrase
such as "Hugh had begun to dote"
will weigh as a Clydesdale's withers would weigh with withies

while the pied wagtail crossing freshly turned furrows
is a tiny rowboat
glimpsed now and again in the trough between storm-waves.

AMERICAN STANDARD

1

Not for nothing would I toil through Manhattan Valley on the
    very horse
I'd "borrowed" (if you get my drift),
from the gymkhana-mad daughter of a rum heiress

I met on the night shift
in Balthazar. The face at my left stirrup
pushed and shoved

along my thigh. A child's face, but worn. A leather strop.
His mouth a razor.
"*Por favor*," he said. "Sorry to disturb

you but I'll need your steed." He needed, too, to reassure
me I'd have him back just as soon as they returned from San
    Antone.
"San Antone?" "They picked us up at Rosario's,

my brother and me, and he's still detained
in the Center on South Laredo."
"How do you come to be so far north?" "I slipped out through
    Anodyne.

4

The guards had given us a PlayStation 4. They weren't alert
to the fact we could escape
by our own devices. Check out this lariat

I made from the lid of a jar of Super Chunk Skippy.
It should fit our steed nicely, though it might be ever so
    slightly snug."
"Does rescuing a brother fall within your scope?"

"If I can make San Antone without a snag
the rest should be as easy as falling off a log."
That was a phrase my uncle Jim used betimes. He'd worked
    with SNCC

in Mississippi during the hard slog
of voter registration. "Particularly if *Señor* comes along for the
    ride."
My own security had been so slack

the boy had shimmied up behind me on the saddle. His pint-
    sized heart
fluttering at my back. My uncle still spoke of Freedom Summer
when so much else along his life-road

had been lost to Alzheimer's.
A razor-mouth at my ear. The blood-plastered
heads of Schwerner, Goodman, and Chaney. The smash and
    smear

of their pulverized

child-faces. We were heading down Amsterdam at a trot when
    a voice uttered

as a voice had uttered that first night in Balthazar:

"Hello. My name is Virgil and I'll be your waiter.

We offer steak tartare as an appetizer for twenty dollars and
    twenty-eight as a main course.

May I start you off with a little water?"

2

As the first deaths from Hurricane Florence are being reported,
President Donald Trump claims
Hurricane Maria's death toll of near three thousand in Puerto
  Rico
was inflated to cause him political harm.

Co co rico Puerto co co rico

On the Georgia Sea Islands, where white islanders outnumber
  black,
resort development has driven prices so high—
not to speak of the raise in property tax—
many of the locals can no longer afford to stay.

Shanty. Shanty. Shanty.

Highlights of Gullah cuisine include Frogmore Stew, Hoppin'
  John,
Purloo, and Calabash with oysters and clams.
"That's no harness jangle," Virgilio insists, "but the jangle of
  chains
from their ancestors stirring under the palms.

Co co rico co co rico

My own ancestors were Irish. The San Patricios.
I'm proud of all the Irish blood that's in me.
My great-great-grandfather's cheek was branded with a D.
    Deserter.
Divvil a man can say a word agin me."

Chantey. Chantey. Chantey.

A cooked rooster is served to a magistrate.
When someone is brought before him accused of a crime
and the dead cock comes back to life and crows from the plate
this miracle may be taken as proof that the accused is without
    blame.

Co co rico co co ricorso co co rico.

3

What comes around goes around for the ten-ton alligator

that can tear up your tarmacadam drive

while turning on a dime.

Come in

Come in under

Come in under the shadow

of the Red Rocks Amphitheatre

where Trent Reznor only recently performed "The Perfect Drug"

 live

for the first time.

"Virgil. Right? Your waiter.

Tonight we're offering gator-ribs marinated in Colt 45

with a reduction of primeval slime."

It was my own apostle,

Thomas, who put his hand in the vent

in my side so as to banish *my* misgivings. *My* doubts.

Come in

Come in under

Come in under the shadow

of the fossil

of a forty-foot sea serpent

that flourished here 200 million years ago, or thereabouts.

That was back when there was one colossal

supercontinent.

Long before each nation was persuaded it had some clout.

The fact that I offered the pediluvy

of my disciples as a proof of my selflessness

would often translate to a much bigger tip.

Come in

Come in under

Come in under the shadow

cast by *Lost Highway*, yet another movie

that's at once a masterpiece and a mess,

and into the soundtrack of which "The Perfect Drug" was

    slipped.

Oh groovy, groovy, groovy.

We drank absinthe with sugar cubes till the road of excess

ran alongside an eight-lane Möbius strip.

The fact is it's the washed-up, the whack-jobs, the world-weary

who are most likely to prevail

in the current zeitgeist.

Come in

Come in under

Come in under the shadow

of that little dune, that former foothill of Dhaulagiri,

its meld of igneous and sedimentary shale.
In *Lost Highway* the characters of Pete and Fred are similarly
    "spliced."
One likable, if unlikely, theory
is that Trent Reznor's band name, Nine Inch Nails,
refers to the crucifixion of Christ.

A half-empty carton of eggs in Luby's Cafeteria
in San Antone brought to mind the mud-loving dinosaur
and the evolution of its open nest.
Come in
Come in under
Come in under the shadow
of the Jurassic period and the rise of the Eutheria,
such animals as bore
their offspring in a womb and clutched them to their breasts.
That was back in the day when a refugee from Syria
might easily have been cast ashore
in the American west.

4

We'd landed up outside Luby's on the way to the junior prom.
There was myself, Ezra, and Tom.
I was wearing my party dress.
Ezra said that he was a great believer in less
being more. His blue pencil was always at the ready.
The pair of them were slightly unsteady
on their legs. They must have been drinking Cherry Bombs
and now imagined we were in a rom-com
when, in fact, we were in *Rambo III*.
Next thing I knew Tom claimed to be quoting John Donne.
Only if I let him put a finger in me
would he know I was the One.

The limo driver glanced back from his cage
while Tom and Ezra the Scribe eyed me like a blank page
on which they might yet make their marks.
A strange name for a limo company. Shark.
Before I knew it they were on top of me. I was pinned under.
While *Perkwunos*, the Indo-European god of thunder,
is at the root of *Quercus*, *Quercus virginiana* seems to reflect the age
of Elizabethan plunderers. In the midst of the sage

stood a *Quercus virginiana*, a single live oak tree.
I was in shock. I'd been hit by a stun gun.
Only if I let him put a finger in me
would he know I was the One.

I remember, as we passed the Mudslingers Drive-Thru,
the uproarious laughter between the two
and their having fun at my expense.
I somehow managed to escape. A picket fence
gave way to the road on which the man I took for a vagrant
turned out to be fragrant
with aloes and myrrh. Even now no one believes that what I say
    is true.
They claim we stopped at Luby's for chocolate Yoo-Hoos.
The pair of them are still laughing uproariously.
Just frat boy stuff. Just having a little fun.
Only if I let him put a finger in me
would he know I was the One.

5

The pocket gopher, like all gophers, has borrowed its name
from *gaufre*, "a honeycomb."

Such is its capacity for burrowing under a live oak
it might well have toppled Rome.

It turns out San Antonio de Padua was born in Lisbon.
No wonder he's the patron saint of Loss.

Tonight Virgilio and I will sleep on gunnysacks
stuffed with Spanish moss.

The pocket gopher is a tunnel within a tunnel.
Get a load of the cheek pouch!

The live oak rests on one elbow
like a Roman king on his verdant couch.

The Roman legionaries were renowned for digging pitfalls
that would give way under an enemy's steed.

The Roman king was known to feast
on dormice marinated in honey and poppy seed.

They reckon a pocket gopher, in the course of a year,
will shift two or three tons of soil.

The live oak seems to favor blond highlights.
Each year the hair salons of the world dump 195 million tons
    of foil.

The U.S. Supreme Court has ruled that the Republican-led
    Legislature in Texas improperly used race
to draw a predominantly Hispanic House district in Fort Worth.

The division between Democrats and Republicans still partly
    reflects
what's known by some as the War Between the States.
The thing about silencing debate is that it cuts down on a lot of
    the back-and-forth.

The Supreme Court overturned a lower court ruling
that invalidated other legislative and congressional districts
    under challenge
for allegedly diluting the voting power of black and Latino
    voters.

What's all that mewling and puking?
Since it has rarely to do with righting a wrong or correcting an
    imbalance
the urge to gerrymander is rarely the urge of an honest broker.

The 5–4 decision, written by Justice Samuel Alito,
leaves in place much of Texas's political map for the 2018
    midterm elections,
upholding political boundaries that have been under court
    review for nearly a decade.

I take a frontiersman as my alter ego
in the shortly-to-be-released prequel to *Red Dead Redemption*.
He wasn't so much of Ulster-Scots background as Huguenot,
    Davy Crockett.

One of the congressional districts under challenge in Texas
is Congressional District 35.
It runs from Austin to San Antonio in the shape of a 200-
    million-year-old sea serpent.

Uncle Jim says we need no help from the Russians when it
    comes to rigging elections.
Virgilio's mother lives in a district contorted to within an inch
    of its life.
The toilet she's wiping down is an American Standard.

7

I'd already gone cap in hand to the rum heiress (Stetson,
   maybe, rather than cap),
to bankroll the western I was developing with Pat McCabe

but she balked at the idea our remake of *A Fistful of Dollars*
might be shot underwater. Even though she knew I'd have a
   firm hand on the tiller

she was concerned about the negative impact on the coral
of the Florida Keys and, more specifically, the logistical
   problems of a sea horse corral.

In this case, she was more than happy to underwrite
our putting together a crack team for the assault on the
   facility on South Laredo.

Virgilio had already signed up his mother, Uncle Jim, and Jim
   Bowie,
and had calls out to Billy Bones, Blind Pew,

Annie Oakley, the English setter she used in her most famous
  sharpshooting routine,
Father Michael Muldoon (who, in 1837, had helped William
  Wharton

escape in the guise of a nun
from the prison in Matamoros), Calamity Jane, and the Lee
  Van Cleef of *High Noon*.

8

Although his uncle may have dealt in arms
that sure don't mean a body's safe from harm.
The killers of Khashoggi musta had nerves of steel
when they stopped him from showin' a clean pair of heels.
They shoulda known things ain't gonna turn out right
if you bring a saw to a fistfight.

At Hidalgo, Texas, U.S. troops are deploying concertina wire
to protect the country from a migrant caravan.
Every plot of waste ground is filled with guns for hire,
guano spotters, Middle Easterners, swarms of ragged ruffians.

Did he take the fact his uncle dealt in arms
as some kinda good luck charm?
The killers of Khashoggi musta had it in their heads
they were close to bein' the sharpest tools in the shed.
They shoulda known things ain't gonna turn out right
if you bring a saw to a fistfight.

Though it was handed down to us from Sinai's spire
we should not make an image that may be described as "graven"

the fact that Christ was caught in his own cross fire
means he's sometimes represented as a lion-bird—a gryphon.

Although his uncle may have dealt in arms
that don't ne'ssarily mean he shoulda bought the farm.
The killers of Khashoggi were slow to recognize
they were s'posed only to cut him down to size.
They shoulda known things ain't gonna turn out right
if you bring a bone-saw to a fistfight.

9

By the mud walls of an ancient city, where Escort Drive runs
     into Sunup,
a construction worker finds a packet wrapped in clear
plastic and lined with Egyptian papyrus.
A frog chorus. Backup beepers.
As for the dog that lies by the gate,
you may be sure the horse at whose heels he's wont to snap
is a horse of a whole other color.

The idea of the superhero's mask and cape goes back to
     Zorro's.
Not that Zorro's cape was sewn with sequins.
The word *zecchino*, by the way, was a term for the Venetian
     gold ducat.
I've never trusted the superhero's impulse to do good.
As for the dog that lies by the gate,
however attached he may once have been to Lazarus and his
     sores
he now prefers Science Diet Sensitive Stomach and Skin.

What I do recall is the bare shoulder

of a young woman in the belly of a Shark limo

and the dim but distinct smell of turf

from that packet found where Sunup transmutes into Escort
    Drive.

As for the dog that lies by the gate,

he remembers nothing of his months in the shelter

never mind the Alamo.

It's the same bush. Some call it greasewood. Some creosote.

It was on June 13, 1691, this shallow plash

was named after the smooth-talking San Antonio de Padua.

"Will that be Perrier?" Virgilio pipes up. "Perrier or Badoit?"

As for the dog that lies by the gate,

he's a lot less prepared for the second coming of Christ

than had seemed at first blush.

The virgins, though, will be trimming their wicks.

They'll have made ready the upper room.

The trumpet shall sound even as the guests are settling at the
    table

and the dead shall be raised incorruptible.

As for the dog that lies by the gate,

you may be sure his head is a whole other ball of wax.

His heart is a whole other can of worms.

10

In the 2018 midterms, the 35th Congressional District has
    gone to Lloyd Doggett,
running yet again on that doggone do-good
Democratic ticket.

Come in
Come in under
Come in under the shadow

of the blue wave running down a urinal at JFK
where, day after day,
Virgilio's mother, Verónica, works a second job. She has
    labored in vain
to wipe out a housefly baked into the porcelain.

A rat creeps softly through the vegetation.
The wind sock on the runway. That's what passes for passion.
A wind sock on the runway gives but little sense of the wind's
    ambition.

Come in
Come in under
Come in under the shadow

of Delta 370 to San Antone.
Virgilio is remarkably composed, given this is the first time he's
    flown.
The rum heiress has moved on from absinthe to Pernod
and is displaying a touch of braggadocio.

David Bowie, meanwhile, has docked
on the River Walk and is securing his glistening, three-hulled
    dugout
when a voice calls from across the duckweed.

Come in
Come in under
Come in under the shadow

of the rum heiress's life vest.
Throughout all this Virgilio has had my back. I am an egg in his
    open nest.
His breath smells of nicotine and licorice.
"Pardon, *Señor*, but do you have any food allegories?"

Come in
Come in under
Come in under the shadow

of the two-party system,

the failure of which seems more and more ad rem

now the archers are ranged against

each other like two ditches, both barbed-wire-fenced.

Lloyd Doggett swears by Hill Country Lavender Goat Milk Body
     Lotion.

"My name," says Lloyd, "my name is Legion."

As far back as 1996, he beat out a Republican, Teresa Doggett
     (no relation).

11

Through fire and flood we rode towards Paradise
where every disaster's a natural disaster
and every word a word of advice
from the ringleted Buffalo Bill, our ringmaster.

Santee. Santee. Santee.

Every wind is a wind that freshens.
Every shock is an aftershock.
Every digression began as a brief digression
and every clock is an alarm clock.

Shandy. Shandy. Shandy.

For every opinion is a public opinion
when every cheek is cheek by jowl
and every minion a bend-me-over minion
just as every barn is possessed of a barn owl.

Shinto. Shinto. Shinto.

Though every true owl is an Athenian
and every god a godsend
every marriage is a marriage of convenience.
Every friend is a fair-weather friend.

Shantee. Shantee. Shantee.

Now every mortgage is a mortgage to the hilt
for the woman who's transgender.
Every quilt is a patchwork quilt.
Every offender is a repeat offender.

Cento. Cento. Cento.

1 2

I have seen the eternal footman hold my coat and knickers
while I took the enchanting East River air.
As I strike out with Father Muldoon and Barbecue
in David Bowie's perilous three-hulled canoe
Je pense à la négresse
who bowdlerized Baudelaire.

It has to be said, in the matter of the perm,
every streak is a losing streak.
"Pardon, *Señor*, but there was something askew
from the day and hour I ran into you.
Manhattan Valley? Don't you know that term
has no currency? It's realtor-speak.

For every abode is no fixed abode.
Every doctor has it in her to make at least one house call.
Just as each of us now gets to choose
whatever might be the most appropriate news.
Just as every area has an area code
I become a transparent eyeball; I am nothing; I see all.

To have any truck with Emerson may be tantamount
to denying the slayer is slain.
The downside of running a second unit, as Henry Wilcoxon knew,
is trying to figure out what Cecil B. would do.
For every fly is a fly in the ointment
though it be engraved in porcelain.

Now every hunger is a spiritual hunger
and every cough a persistent cough
that signals the soul may shortly break through
to a place where things are only slightly out of true.
Ô Mort, vieux capitaine, il est temps! levons l'ancre!
Oh, Death, old captain, hoist the anchor! Come, cast off!

Off with that wiry Coronet and shew the hairy Diadem.
La plus belle des ruses du Diable
isn't only that he manages to feed the cast and crew
on Super Chunk Skippy and Frogmore Stew
c'est qu'il nous faut consentir à toutes les forces extrêmes
like a patient oysterized upon a table."

13

When Trent Reznor performs David Bowie's "I'm Afraid of
   Americans"
he hits it out of the park.
I say "David Bowie." I mean David Jones.
David Jones took the name Bowie from the character portrayed
   by Richard Widmark

in *The Alamo*. The last five times I've flown
I've been selected for a random security search.
Many of my friends reckon
it's because I've made so much of the relationship between the
   Coptic church

and early Irish monasticism. Saint Anthony of Egypt
is not to be confused with our own Anthony of Padua, who had
   such a gift of the gab
his tongue remains imperishable.
Annie Oakley was able to hit a target smack-dab

in the middle of the Chapel
Perilous while (1) shooting over her shoulder and (2) using a
   Bowie knife

as a mirror. It was only as I lay in Nicodemus's crypt

I came to understand that the half-life

of the myrrh Balthazar first offered me in Bethlehem

is a good thirty-three years.

I'm sitting in 12D, right? That means Virgilio must be in 13D.

Only last week, in the Mudslingers Drive-Thru, an old coot in

an '89 Cavalier

embarked on an all-too-familiar threnody.

A porpoise snored upon the phosphorescent swell.

Vis-à-vis Trump, we have only ourselves to blame for giving

ourselves over to pablum.

A triton rang the final warning bell.

14

Not

Not for

Not for nothing

do we remember that we seem to have said good riddance

to what was meant to be our children's inheritance.

We'd hoped they might fetch some flax

and whites of eggs to apply to an eye in flux,

a compound eye giving back the pixelation

of a world that self-destructs even as it comes into being.

The fact is that's the legacy of all heirs-in-waiting, including

the eight D'Ascoynes.

A fly is no less fated to be a denizen

of a jar of myrrh or aloes than a so-called "monk" parakeet

is fated to be a denizen of Jamaica, Queens.

Some presidents seem to say "hi."

Some presidents seem to say "howdy."

Some are in bed with a Soviet spy.

Some are still in bed with the Saudis.

Some of us are still trying to figure out why George W. Bush

would bestow

the favor of stowing away on a plane to thirteen bin Ladens.

We all know that if you spend time in the stew
your goose will be cooked like a goose in Baden-Baden.

Not
Not for
Not for nothing
did we lend an ear to the rooster crowing that third time
for the Jew-bashing Ezra and Tom.
"Pardon, *Señor*, but can't you see that getting a Facebook 'like'
is as easy as falling off a log
when Agni, the god of fire, may take as his locus
the wild iris or the wild crocus?
The fact is Agni's confused with the man-bird, Garuda, known
    to bear ambrosia
to the other gods of the Aryans.
I'm reminded of how, in *Kind Hearts and Coronets*,
Alec Guinness plays all eight D'Ascoyne family members."

Some presidents surround themselves with lickspittles.
Some surround themselves with lackeys.
Some snack on peanut brittle.
Some snack on wacky baccy.
Some of us aren't sure if it's "bestowal" or "bestowment."
We're all of us desperately trying to weigh
the moment of the moment.
"Pardon, *Señor*, but the best cure for a colloquial horse is a touch
    of Say Whoa."

Not

Not for

Not for nothing

do we worry that even the mildest critics

of Israel's domestic policies are characterized as being anti-
    Semitic.

Last week I overheard a girl in Shake Shack

explain how the word *shiksa*

means "off the menu." Now we must each take a position.

Now we have something like a go-situation.

The fact is, as we ready ourselves for the charge,

there's a tension reminiscent of the tension

down in the Venice *borghetto*

that time Tom and Ezra snuck by in their limo-barge.

Some presidents love a big-ass motorcade.

Some don't mind the repercussions

of going to bed without having drawn the shades.

Some are still in bed with the Russians.

Some of us like to worship, then kill, the fatted calf.

Some of us like to keep our diet varied.

Some of us know that Orson Welles sawed Rita Hayworth in
    half.

Some of us know where the bodies are buried.

Not

Not for

Not for nothing

did I set out to be seen to eat broiled fish and honeycomb

but to prove that I was back in the game.

I am the third who walks

between you and Zorro, between you and the Swamp Fox.

So far as I can make out the world has always been a

    hodgepodge, a hocus-pocus

that never quite comes into focus.

The fact is that the new orthodoxies are the old orthodoxies,

what with the rerun

of water cannons and tear gas grenades

along the border from California through Arizona to Texas.

Some presidents' attempts to make America great

are less than gratifying.

Some presidents are lying in state.

Some are plain ol' lying.

Some of us have already taken off from LaGuardia with

    Southwest.

The Swamp Fox is set upon finally draining the swamp.

Some of us will don a yellow vest

at the Washington Monument as at the Arc de Triomphe.

Not

Not for

Not for nothing

do we despair of the idea that, however much we once felt
    rooted,
we're all now disinherited.
"*Los Desheredados*. That's why every man jack
of us has a D branded on the cheek.
That's why it's a D we fly on our ensign.
That's why *Red Dead 2* is the nearest we'll get to redemption."
The fact is, as the rum heiress has often remarked, when it
    comes to a finale,
it's hard to beat the recording of Alfred, Lord Tennyson,
reading "The Charge of the Light Brigade,"
recently reissued on vinyl.

15

When it comes to a finale it's hard to beat the combined
    forces of Buddy Bolden,
Captain Beefheart, the recently cashiered Cap'n Crunch,
Charlemagne and his twelve paladins,
William Tell, William Holden
and the Wild Bunch,

Cyrano de Bergerac, Anthony Burgess,
Frank Zappa, Frank Wedekind,
Jorge Luis Borges, the Borgias,
the Man in Black, the Thin White Duke, My Last Duchess,
    Preston Sturges,
Buffalo Bill, P. T. Barnum, Jenny Lind,

Bennie and the Jets, Bernardo Bertolucci,
Bernard of Clairvaux in the Vallée d'Absinthe,
Pocahontas, John Smith, Joseph Smith, the prophet Elijah,
Amelia Earhart, Emily Dickinson, Émile Zola, Emiliano Zapata,
    Emilio Pucci,
the Duke of Aquitaine (a.k.a. John of Gaunt),

Sister Sara who long ago gave up the cloister

for life with two mules,

Maria Tallchief, the Tailor of Gloucester,

Ralph Vaughan Williams, our friend Ralph Waldo Emerson,

    Ralph Roister Doister,

Nancy Cunard, the New York School,

an ever more erratic Uncle Jim, Davy Crockett

and his faux coonskin hat,

Jimi Hendrix, Jiminy Cricket,

April Bloomfield, Anthony Bourdain, Kermit the Frog, Toad the

    Wet Sprocket,

Jelly Roll Morton, Jumping Jehoshaphat,

Calamity Jane, Annie Oakley,

Alicia Keys, the Keystone Kops,

St. Vincent, Saint Cecilia, Cecilia Fire Thunder and an elite war

    band of Oglala,

the Carmichaels Hoagy and Stokely,

not to mention a Special Ops

division comprising El Chapo, Robin Hood, Harry Houdini,

    and Zorro.

As we're pushing away from the gate

the Man in Black is heard to remark to Sister Sara

and a Man of Constant Sorrow

that a red-and-white striped sock will surely help our archers

    compensate

for wind speed and direction. The Teenage Mutant Ninja Turtles
needn't mind losing their reputation for being tight-lipped.
Nor need we mind the serial ordeal
of being watched by forty cellular phones as we hurtle
along the dimly lit South Laredo, worried mostly our steed
    might be tripped

in a hole engineered by such pocket
gophers as have gone over to the other side.
"Pardon, *Señor*, but what the worker found in the packet
at Sunup and Escort was an Irish Psalter wrapped in the
    screenplay for *Bottle Rocket*."
Virgilio still has my back. "That's where I got the idea I should
    slide

down a sheet when making my escape." Macmorris and his
    petard hoisters
are augmented now by Kurt Weill, Kurt Vonnegut,
Buckethead the shredder, the shredder Banksy, Castor and
    Pollux, Lady Astor,
Lady Hamilton, Nelson Rockefeller, a half dozen West Coast
    oysters,
the 7th Cavalry, Slattery's Mounted Fut,

Omar the Tentmaker, Amerigo Vespucci,
Nico, Nicolas Roeg,
the Man Who Fell to Earth, Geronimo, Hieronymus Bosch,

Mad Max, Muddy Waters doing the hoochie-coochie
with Lewis and Clark in their three-hulled pirogue,

Guy of Gisbourne, Guy Burgess,
Aretha Franklin, Edward Longshanks,
Patti Smith, the San Patricios, a snatch squad of Brigantes in
    their distinctive britches,
Frank Zappa himself desperate for the slightest purchase
on the steep bank

of breaking news, Conan O'Brien cohosting our brutal
assault with Conan the Barbarian even as Sir Arthur Conan
    Doyle's
assuring us our hope we might gain access to the Detention
    Center by way of *Bridge Constructor Portal*
on PlayStation 4 isn't entirely futile,
assuring us it's not entirely for nothing we toil.

A RUIN

It might have been a gristmill, a dilapidated granary, or grange
I first drove by some sixty years ago
and, with my little eye, espied
through a doorframe the tousled ferns
and red-haired dockens
of kids my own age sent out to play in the snow,
their snowballs
so specific in the sprawl.
Windowless now, roofless, tucked

under the first, sheltering hill of a range
that ran all the way to Mexico—
a country into which we still hoped to ride
hell-for-leather, still hoped to adjourn
after the stickup—this ruin betokens
not only the slo-mo-
mowing of a meadow for a shopping mall
but the fate that would befall
the many tagged and retagged

over those sixty years. The landscape is so marked by change,
the bungled peace process, the shoddy bungalows,
the wind farms taking us in their stride,

so marked by all the turns

things have indeed taken

for kids now summoned back from playing in the snow,

the nettles almost as tall

as its dividing wall,

a ruin seems the only thing intact.

SHOOT 'EM UP

I don't suppose a bandit often achieves his goal
of swapping a bedroll for lath and plaster.
Many's a storefront has caved in. Crumpled like a blouse.
Rarely is a mainstay made manifest.

That's why I check out each and every gopher hole
for the mink stole that eluded J. J. Astor.
The varmints back in the boardinghouse?
They, too, wanted to pin a star on my chest.

I don't suppose a piano is ever quite in tune.
That's why a piano player will precipitously change course
when a version of himself comes to pass

through the doors of the saloon.
That's why bandits keep barging in and out two-to-a-horse
through windows made of sugar-glass.

DAMSONS

Alas, good master, my wife desired some damsons
And made me climb, with danger of my life.
—Simpcox, *Henry VI, Part 2*

1

It would take more than a clip round the ear
to bring me to my senses
as I tried to get clear
what exactly a United Ireland would mean to my next-door
     neighbor.
His trench coat had been made by Thomas Burberry.
The last time I'd seen him he'd presented me with a pot of jam
     for my journey
and a rumpled copy of *The Big Sleep*.

2

I'd set out that morning fortified by the aroma
of Nescafé that must have wafted over from as far away as
     Brannigan's.

I knew flax-holes were bogholes with linnets.

I knew Uncle Pat's Ford Prefect was a donkey cart with a
    motor.

3

I also knew that, in June 1954, the IRA had raided Gough
    Barracks in Armagh

and made off with a lorry-load of Sten and Bren guns.

The myxoma virus was introduced to Ireland that same
    summer.

When we'd moved from Eglish to Collegelands

these damson trees were already mature.

Even though we'd now lived here for five years we were still
    newcomers.

4

It would take more than a clip round the ear

to assuage my lifelong fear

of stretches of bog-road like the one outside Urney

where we'd been stopped by soldiers in what I took for Jeeps.

In a novel by Raymond Chandler

a man may never lower his defenses

as he climbs towards the chandelier

to the accompaniment of tambourine and tabor.
When would I be done with the tuppenny world, the turbary?
It would take more than a clip round the ear
to bring me to my senses.

5

By the time I'd heard of "A Coney Island of the Mind"
I knew it wasn't the Coney Island to which Pat had driven us a
    mere ten miles.
My mother had told me flax was pulverized
by boys who insisted on being boys.

6

As I'd set out I had a cheer of encouragement
from another neighbor on his way to work in the Moygashel
    linen mills.
Although I'd seen many of their kind die of myxomatosis
I'd acquired two fresh rabbits in Belfast.
I was equipped with a parachute, needless to say, and my
    recurve bow.
The technical term for my mother's drooping eyelids was
    ptosis.

7

As I tried to get clear
of the world of seed-surges and menses
so many held so dear
I carried that pot of jam and a sense of life being worthless.
I was still trying to fathom
why I should be attending the ritual cleansing at the altar
of a woman who had recently given birth.

8

I can't say I expected to move in the same orbit
as Yuri Gagarin, now I'd managed to kick away the ladder,
but I would have been glad to share the cloudberries left in
    the punnet
I'd gathered from a north-facing slope in Mullaguttural.

9

One of the big dangers in keeping rabbits
is that the doe is more likely than not to eat her litter.
We kept them in separate hutches under the row of damsons.
From this vantage point

I could see Armagh and the twin spires of St. Patrick's
    Cathedral.
The story went the IRA man who led the raid was carrying a
    Thompson.

10

I was still trying to get clear
why Macha's charioteer
had dandled a Barbary ape imported from Gibraltar
when he should have been tightening the pony's girth.
In a novel by Raymond Chandler
a man may charge twenty-five dollars a day plus expenses
as he climbs towards the chandelier.
Here I would still wear an altar boy's soutane and surplice
and hover like his own phantasm
as he tried to get clear
of the world of seed-surges and menses.

11

The constant friction
In Northern Ireland made the term "Orange Free State" seem
    nuts

yet Larry Toal had an Orange Free State stamp complete with
    its original gum.
There was little likelihood Catholics would ever achieve parity.

12

I may have started climbing because I'd been slapped for some
    minor infraction.
Not the little slap Bacall gives Bogart in *To Have and Have Not.*
More like the slap Gunnar gives Hallgerdhur in *Njal's Saga.*
Hard to believe that in years to come
I would drive Lauren Bacall home from a New York party.
Larry Toal had heard the National Museum of Ireland owned a
    stuffed quagga.

13

What the parishioners held dear
was the idea there would be no consequences
for giving someone a clip round the ear.
When would I ever be done with the effrontery
of a clip round the ear or a slap in the dial
from the parish priest for having suggested that a three-leaf
    clover
represented the Trinity as one flesh?

14

As time went by, my mother would take to singing "The Lonely
   Goatherd."
The chances of finding a springbok
in the National Museum were about as strong
as finding a beatnik on a bog-road between Ballybofey and
   Lifford.

15

The small crowd that had by now gathered
was almost equally divided between spurring me on and
   ordering me back.
I loved how Halderdhur would later deny Gunnar
a strand of her hair to replace his broken bowstring.
My parachute straps had been made at Moygashel as part of the
   war effort.
The damsons were themselves notorious for sending out
   runners.

16

What the crowd holds dear
is the notion there'll be no reckoning in the political sphere.

In August 1971 my neighbor would be bundled into an army
    Land Rover
and installed in a new prison in Long Kesh.
Surely it's not only in a novel by Raymond Chandler
that a body tenses?
Even as I climbed towards the amber chandelier
the Unionists, almost as an involuntary
response, had introduced internment without trial.
What they held dear
was the idea
there would be no consequences.

BRAMLEYS, NOT GRENADIERS

The apple trees are put up against a wall
and shot at dawn.
The bodies lie where they fall.
These are Armagh Bramleys, not Grenadiers,
given their russet tinge.
That's blood coming out of an ear.
At the heart of the espalier is the stake
to which the branches are bound with pantyhose
to allow for a little give-and-take.
The apple trees are put up against a wall
almost as often as, in Gaelic football,
Maghery is bested by the boys of Mullaghbawn.
These are Armagh Bramleys, not Grenadiers
for whom the thought of pruning shears
will cause a twinge.
At the heart of the espalier is the stake
about which Grenadiers are known to bellyache.
That's blood coming out of a nose.
The apple trees put up against a wall
and shot at dawn
are Armagh Bramleys, not Grenadiers,
given their russet tinge.
At the heart of the espalier is the stake
to which the branches are bound with pantyhose.

23 BANNED POEMS

1. ANONYMOUS: *LE MIRACLE DE LA RÉSURRECTION DES POULETS RÔTIS* (1470)

Not only brined but brined
and trussed

with butcher's twine,
his blood taking more than one slot

in the cutting board, transfixed
then on a spit

and granted a vision
of Hell forsooth.

When Mary saw Longinus peruse
his gear

and choose
not the poultry shears

but the trussing needle a bruise
had suddenly appeared

on her breast as if it was she whose
breast was seared.

Seasoned with lemon rind,
paprika dust,

and a ton
of salt,

Jesus hangs betwixt
and between a rock and a soft spot

while the mob, in typical fashion,
is all simmer and seethe.

As Mary braces
herself against their jeers

she knows Jesus
is done, or near,

when Longinus pierces
his side with a spear

and the juices
at last run clear.

2. LEONARDO DA VINCI:
THE LAST SUPPER (1495-98)

"It's from that other Mary, the Magdalene,
they've borrowed the bedsheet
that doubles as a tablecloth. So clean.
So neat."

"Except for the crease
that will become a San Andreas Fault.
A gutter filled with candle grease.
The semen stain where Judas spilled his salt."

3. HIERONYMUS BOSCH: *THE TEMPTATION OF SAINT ANTHONY* (1501)

No sign in this case of the *Tau*, the Greek letter T
so familiar to Tory islanders.
That *Tau* is Anthony's emblem.

No sign of the hollow tree
where he lives. A tree part cunt, part O'Neill cylinder.
No sign of the Egyptian plum

with its own cleft. Still
no sign of his pig, the proto-Landrace.
There is, however, a demon-bird on ice skates

with a placard fixed on one crossed bill.
"The leaves of the oleander,"
it might read, "are lethal to goats,

camels, and sheep."
It might be a page flying off a calendar
in *I Am a Fugitive from a Chain Gang*. But it wrong-foots

Anthony with a backwards jab

at his being so slender

on account of the vicissitudes of desert life: "Fatso."

4. RAPHAEL: *MADONNA OF THE GOLDFINCH* (1505)

That's John the Baptist got up in a leather loincloth.
Geomancer. Trailblazer.
Cutter of a swath

through artemisia. Curtain-raiser
for the main act.
Precursor of the great stargazer

across a contested tract.
Needle-threader. Stitcher of camel hair trousers.
Accessory after the fact

to rogues and rabble-rousers.
Straight man to your Man.
Each in his way a goldfinch, a browser

on his own spiked brainpan.
One a lover of locusts and wild honey.
The other no less a loser. An also-ran

in his seamless cloak of straw and gunny.
Given the goldfinch's predilection for prickles,
Raphael would be right on the money

were he to afford the Christ-child a sickle
in anticipation of the gathering in.
The goldfinch's red? Where he took the trickle

of Christ's blood, took it on the chin.
He'd do it again, he would, for two pins.
The gold flakes Caligula will feed his horse? Flakes of whin

mixed with bran from the provender bin.
Remember, a "horse" will froth
at the bit only when it's happy in its skin.

5. LUCAS VAN LEYDEN: *THE MILKMAID* (1510)

It needs someone of the stature of Massimo Bovenzi
to calibrate the scale
of the frenzy
with which this milkmaid last night stirred
the milk in her wooden pail
till, under the watchful eye of two serving wenches,
it separated into spunk-whey and spunk-curds.

Those curds have been known to provision
one of those little platoons
of Poor Clares. Whereas a speaker of Old Frisian
will almost absentmindedly peel
a yew-stick in order to notch up a rune,
it's with grim determination a Mother Superior quenches
her flame with a freshwater eel.

Nor is the eel the only slippery customer
who entertains both the glaur
and the gossamer
in a world where so much tends to homogenize.
That cock, for example, has been awarded the bronze star
for its exploits in the trenches.
Hi, Massimo. Big boy! Why don't you try that for size?

6. MATTHIAS GRÜNEWALD: *THE TEMPTATION OF SAINT ANTHONY* (1512)

It may be "Fatty" or it may be "Fiat" (in the sense of a
    proclamation).
Saint Anthony is, after all, on a mission

to grease the wheals
of ergotism. Of the pig they use "everything but the squeal"

in the rendering of lard
but no one would actually put a lot of stock in the stockyard

till the Earl of Rochester's "Fair Chloris
in a Pigsty Lay" would evince the glorious

from the glaur and glit
and make more nymphs more mindful of their clits.

The sight of one of the devils wearing some sort of apparatus
that offers a shortcut to Paradise

transports me to Rochester, New York, where I once met a
    most likely lass
who liked it mostly in the ass.

7. JAN WELLENS DE COCK: *THE TEMPTATION OF SAINT ANTHONY* (1520)

The patron saint of infectious diseases
still hasn't connected the fact that when he sneezes
a few more Aztecs bite the dust.

In 1432, Eoghan O'Neill had been top banana.
That same year when, according to the Annals, Fermanagh
was ravaged by plague,

the Aztecs had formed an alliance with several city-states.
The emperor wore a quilted breastplate.
His mask was of turquoise, pine resin, and nacre.

Now stout Cortés came riding, armed with a goose gun,
like Moses in search of a prodigal son
for whom to kill the golden calf.

If only Montezuma
had kept that incense burner in the shape of a puma
it might have helped to clear the air.

As it was, the 1520 smallpox epidemic in Tenochtitlán
would make a tree of at least one man
afflicted with leaf rust.

Agnès Sorel was born in 1422. Too young as yet for nipple-rouge.
By 1432 Jan van Eyck had moved to Bruges
from the piss-pot of the Hague

and flourished there among the spinners and weavers,
millies, doffers, true blues, and unbelievers
for whom nothing is sacred.

That Cortés would hold Montezuma and the Aztec nation
in something approaching veneration
is plain as a pikestaff.

What's much less evident
is how van Eyck's depiction of Eve in the 1432 altarpiece in Ghent
had made straight the path to this snaggle of pubic hair.

8. JACOPO TINTORETTO: *SUSANNA AND THE ELDERS* (1555-56)

Two old wankers wont mainly to eavesdrop
on a knocking shop are hoping to spy
on Susanna as she's sousing her roll-mop.
Could be they'll cop an eyeful of her nether eye.

However slim their chances of having her tap
into the sap now rising in their rods
whether she'll even lay her head in one's lap
is totally in the lap of the gods.

9. PLAUTILLA NELLI: *THE LAST SUPPER* (1560)

It took someone who knew what they were doing
to kill that little lamb curled in its plate.
It took someone who knew what they were doing
to paint each shuddering little pleat

in the tablecloth. Each little fuck-fosse
a flat-footed laundress subjected to a weekly bluing.
As for preparing a kosher fish sauce,
that took someone who knew what they were doing.

10. ARTEMISIA GENTILESCHI:
SUSANNA AND THE ELDERS (1610)

When they're rebuffed
the elders accuse Susanna of being herself a wanton,

of strutting her stuff
under a tree. Though some doctors have indeed prescribed
 Zarontin

for *le petit mal*, there's no known cure
for *la petite mort* except perhaps the snipping of the bollocks.

In addition to already having a certain hauteur
Blaise Pascal was very much to the forefront in hydraulics.

In 1646, his father, Étienne, had broken his femur in a fall
and come under the care of two bonesetters

for whom "If you lose, you lose nothing. If you gain, you gain
 all"
was a maxim they shared with most aiders and abettors.

The fine line between faithful and fawning? The English water
    spaniel.
Blaise Pascal is the type who'll wager

that, however sage Daniel
might turn out to be, Susanna will prove even sager

for she has already vowed to lay fresh wormwood to her dug
so any child she suckles

will soon be weaned . . . One old wanker imagines her
    grabbing his lugs
as he rummages through her ruckle.

11. PETER PAUL RUBENS:
PROMETHEUS BOUND (1611)

Now that the eagle has the bit between
her teeth she brings to mind
nothing so much as the night I first laid out a town
on your mound

of Venus. Though most believe Alexander the Great
took his cue from Hippodamus
vis-à-vis the notion of the grid
you preferred to think the Celts devised the oppidum.

Now that the eagle still has the bit between
her teeth she's running with the idea
the language we know as Thracian

(in which, for example, the word for a hillfort is *dún*),
was spoken as recently as the fifth century A.D.
and is ripe, ripe, ripe for regeneration.

12. THOMAS GAINSBOROUGH:
GIRL WITH PIGS (1782)

It's been a downward spiral
ever since humankind went viral
with chickens and pigs.

She first had intimations
of intimate relations
while she was mid-frig.

The cause of her undoing
was the chance of a corkscrewing
by a nose-ringed boar.

Even as he trifles with her ruffles
she rifles through the truffles
in his Périgord.

13. THOMAS COLE:
PROMETHEUS BOUND (1846-47)

It must have seemed they'd made up ground
when they traded buffalo grass
and a stream kneeling at its trough
and salt flats already cartwheel-grooved

for a world in which they'd sound
out an idea only as it came to them. Whoreglass.
Nepotatoes. Quaff, oh quaff.
Clefsticles like as of fire. Behooved.

When Jacob Donner's body was found
high in that mountain pass
his arms and legs had been artfully hacked off
and his heart and liver removed.

14. FRANCESCO HAYEZ:
SUSANNA AT HER BATH (1850)

When the judge, Daniel, separates the elders
and inquires of the first under which kind of tree Susanna
    sinned, "Alder,"

he ventures. "It was an alder. Or an ash."
"An angel stands ready," says Daniel, "to alter you, to slash

you from stem to stern."
The second elder testifies in his turn,

"It was a pear tree, I'm almost certain. A European pear."
"An angel stands ready," says Daniel, "to pare

the rind off your pith as they pared the rind off Saint
    Bartholomew.
That's how we treat most cases of epithelioma

in this neck of the woods." The second elder comes back with
    "Yew,
was it? Or pine?" "An angel stands ready to hew

a plank from your spine." "Could it have been a chestnut?"
"An angel stands ready to cut

you off in your prime and research the coefficient of drag,"
says Daniel, quietly weighing his options, "on what passes for
    your ball-bag."

15. THOMAS HART BENTON:
SUSANNA AND THE ELDERS (1938)

Cunt is at the nerve center of OB-GYN.
Cunt is your kith and kine.

Cunt is your Sumerian cuneiform.
Cunt is the wedge of a bee-swarm

in the coign
of an arch in the groin.

Cunt is one of the interpenetrating cones
in the midst of which we find one of Yeats's stones.

Cunt is the candidate who's a shoo-in.
Cunt is the haven at Anach Cuan

where a boat with one rotten plank goes down
and nineteen unfortunates drown.

Cunt is the coney burrowing under the wych elm.
Cunt is the coin of the realm.

16. DAVID ARONSON: *THE LAST SUPPER* (1944)

"What happened in the olive grove
that led to our exit being barred?"
saith the Garlic Clove.
"Vengeance is mine," saith the Lard.

"Since when did you give a toss
about saving the shipyard?"
saith the Carrageen Moss.
"Vengeance is mine," saith the Lard.

"And when will it become clear
who moved my place card?"
saith the Asparagus Spear.
"Vengeance is mine," saith the Lard.

"Who serves Arctic char
on a bed of Swiss chard?"
saith Johnny Guitar.
"Vengeance is mine," saith the Lard.

"And who would have guessed
this dump is Michelin-starred?"

saith the Lemon Zest.
"Vengeance is mine," saith the Lard.

"Why did you nip outside for a smoke
with that dishy Praetorian guard?"
saith the Jerusalem Artichoke.
"Vengeance is mine," saith the Lard.

"And why do some still bruit
that widespread canard?"
saith the Horseradish Root.
"Vengeance is mine," saith the Lard.

"Where is the bed that was disturbed
though the frost's still hard?"
saith the Bitter Herb.
"Vengeance is mine," saith the Lard.

17. MAX ERNST: *THE TEMPTATION OF SAINT ANTHONY* (1945)

"Surely an artist in your league
wouldn't sell himself for thirty pieces of wampumpeag?
For some kind of publicity stunt?"

"Your trust in the intrinsic value of being chaste
is somewhat misplaced,
to be perfectly blunt."

"Isn't it enough to have gone half a league, half a league?
Enough simply to have endured the blitzkrieg?
Enough simply to have borne the brunt?"

"When we end up being served pastry-encased
or as a pulled pork sandwich, open-faced,
it's no odds if you're Il Duce or a runt."

"To think the League of Nations were out of their own league.
That so many of us capitulate out of sheer fatigue
at the heels of the hunt."

"Surely to be accused of a minor breach of good taste
when the cities of Europe are laid waste
is an even greater affront?"

18. SALVADOR DALÍ: *THE TEMPTATION OF SAINT ANTHONY* (1946)

"What losses might you ever recoup
when all you've built
is a series of hoops
and a troupe
of elephants on stilts?"

"I don't mind if I'm attacked
by a snatch squad.
I would like, though, to take back
the feelings over which those hacks
have ridden roughshod."

"Don't bother your hole.
You know you're an old-school stylite
whose only goal
was to live atop a pole
of your own shite."

"Nor do I mind if I'm doomed to pay
out my wiggly-wad.

It means that every day
I've come a little way
closer to God."

19. LOUISE BOURGEOIS:
FEMME MAISON (1946-47)

The rooftop garden
of 30 Rockefeller.
A bag of cement that hardens
in a cellar.

Is the woman a house
or the house a woman?

In the nursery
a rocking horse has neighed.
It elicits only a cursory
glance from the upstairs maid.

Is the woman a house
or the house a woman?

The hymnal overruling
Household Hints from the chantry.
A pound cake cooling
in the pantry.

Is the woman a house
or the house a woman?

The constant warble
of those little brown jobs
and, on its corbel,
the crow with which they hobnob.

Is the woman a house
or the house a woman?

At her palace door
a box for a sentry.
A delivery from the dry-goods store
by her back entry.

Is the woman a house
or the house a woman?

20. GEORGIA O'KEEFFE: *PELVIS SERIES* (1947)

Just as her sexuality is "budding"
Susanna's now somewhat chastened
to find she's put all her puddings
in one basin.

Things used to be crystal clear. Clear as crystal.
Now everyone's a layman
in the matter of how the pistil
receives the stamen.

21. LEONORA CARRINGTON:
THE TEMPTATION OF SAINT ANTHONY (1947)

There's still no sign of that poor slob
whose shrieks and sobs
went pretty much unremarked,

who must still throb
from the corncob
Popeye shoved up his bottom quark.

Like that folktale from the Punjab
in which a roast squab
ups and flies from his spit.

What kind of snob
prefers crates to wattle-and-daub?
A Saddleback? A Gloucester Old Spot?

Alexander Selkirk would stick his knob
in the thingamabob
of a nanny goat.

Still no sign of that other poor slob

who ran foul of the mob

and now wears a cement overcoat.

From the kettle a gob

of water skitters across the hob

like a star in the night sky that's erred

on the side of one of those ladies who'll fob

you off with a hand job

instead of going the whole nine yards.

22. JUDY CHICAGO: *THE DINNER PARTY* (1974-79)

When a man is sizing up a snatch
he's a bear sizing up a berry patch

but Richard Nixon had his own wilderness years.

When a woman points to her corner molding
she may be emotionally withholding

but Richard Nixon was known to shed a tear.

When a man is building a fence
it may be because of irreconcilable elements

but Richard Nixon straddled East and West.

When a woman offers you a tipple
she's inviting you to suck her nipples

but Richard Nixon kept things close to his chest.

When most men are checking out a quim
they're envisioning six-winged seraphim

but Richard Nixon kept his feet on the ground.

When a woman offers you seconds
it may be only because she's reckoned

she no longer has Nixon to kick around.

When a man reaches across the fence
he's often inwardly incensed.

Not Richard Nixon. He never was bent out of shape.

When a woman offers you her finest china
she's offering you her own vagina

and Richard Nixon had it all on tape.

23. FERNANDO BOTERO: *ABU GHRAIB* (2005)

It's no exaggeration
to say a sentry at his station
may succumb to mission creep,
acting with such abandon
the prisoner in his keep
doesn't have a leg to stand on.

In this case he'll falter
because the tightening of a halter
is bound to unleash
the memory of Gitmo,
just as finding your niche
may usher in an utter shit-show.

THE DIRTY PROTEST

Though *weregild* and *eric* may both refer to the concept of "a
    blood price"
there are concepts that float free of any word.
Take Peter Bardens, the former keyboardist for Them,
showing up on *Wavelength* in 1978. Is there a term for that? Or
    a farmer of pecans
enjoying a higher status
than a peanut farmer. If allegations of assault were made
    against officers

in the RUC, very rarely were said officers
subject to investigation. In the matter of Alan Price and only
    Alan Price
receiving songwriting credits for "The House of the Rising
    Sun," that special status
reflects the alphabet. In the beginning was the word
and the word was *Bhagwan.*
When I first read Langston Hughes's "Theme

for English B" I had some sense of the concept of being under
    a thumb,
chiefly from my encounters with UDR officers
who were former B-Specials. The Baltimore Beacon

was built in the light of 1798; although a United Ireland was a
    pearl of great price
those who cherished that idea were often, in a word,
terrorists. In early Irish society, chieftains and other men of
    status

were buried standing up, like their own statues,
their faces set against their enemies. By 1978 "Moondance"
    was an anthem
Van Morrison played twice on one night in the Bottom Line.
    Their names a byword
for militant Republicanism to the officers
in Armagh Gaol, the sisters Dolours and Marian Price
were trying to keep their noses clean. The Israeli Prime
    Minister, Menachem Begin,

had signed another peace treaty with the Piegan
around the time Earl Old Person was granted the honorary
    status
of Chief of the Blackfeet. All for the price
of a blanket! That arrhythmia may be cured by a self-
    administered chest thump
is well attested by officers
of all stripes. On that you have not only their word

but Jimmy Carter's. As far back as 1976, the IRA leaders in the
    Maze had sent word

to the Army Council asking them to begin
a campaign of assassinating prison officers.
The idea was that since the prisoners were prepared to die for
    political status,
those who tried to take it away from them
must be prepared to pay the same price.

Who would have guessed that every god, pagan or Christian,
    has his price?
Or that an Irish king might keep, as a status symbol, a Viking
    sword?
Who would have guessed that lithium would be such a money-
    spinner for Pfizer?

A POSTCARD FROM SAINT BART'S

An Elvis impersonator
curling his lip
as he limbers up for "Return to Sender,"
a wave may develop

that slight curling of the lip
till it becomes a sneer.
Not that a wave may more than slightly develop.
The character of Snare

becomes a sneer
no less than Master Fang,
the character of Snare
being in a funk

no less than his buddy, Master Fang.
Pretending to be a havoc-wreaker
while being in a blue funk
is pretty much de rigueur

since your typical havoc-wreaker
doesn't have the chops.
It's pretty much de rigueur
for the sea to take out a few ships

unless it doesn't have the chops.

Unless it can't rise to the occasion.

For a self-respecting sea to take out a few ships

is a sine qua non

just as being confident he'll rise to the occasion

while limbering up for "Return to Sender"

is a sine qua non

for the white-pearled Elvis impersonator.

MAYDAY

1

The desert would be an ocean were it able to withhold
its judgment on wavelet after sand-wavelet
and suspend itself over its own floor.

2

It's not only death's a Great Leveler.

3

The desert has its own version of spume,
its own version of spindrift—
that flurry of grains by the wavelet-crest.

4

My email somehow ended up in your spam.
I hope you know it was only a rough draft.

5

Though it may be twelve thousand years old, the creosote,
it's not the pitch Noah used, in the Flood,
to keep his tanker afloat.

6

Then there's that other desert plant for which to flower
is to signal distress—to send up a distress flare.

ANONYMOUS: THE VIKINGS

It's keen as a sword's edge, the wind tonight.
The sea-mane an unruly shock of white.
It means a raiding party of the Norse
would almost certainly be blown off-course.

CLEGS AND MIDGES

1

The fact that Socrates is represented by Aristophanes
as a gadfly tormenting the body politic in some political horse
    barn or byre
only stiffens

my resolve to raise the bar
back at the milking parlor. Taking their name from the Viking
term for a "burr,"

clegs have a way of spiking
a story whilst splashing it all over the front page.
I'll be damned if I'll let them come within striking

distance of my home patch.
The green of the cesspool is the green of ceremonial-grade
    matcha.
Having made a botch

of my exposed forearms, the clegs now mooch
about the hindquarters of a heifer.
The bullock that had long since seemed to have lost his mojo

takes off across the water meadow like a zephyr.

Since I am no longer wont

to be targeted as Chilon the Ephor

was targeted by his fellow Spartans, when it comes to sustaining
    wounds

the clegs and I are pretty much even-steven.

The midges, in the meantime, have thrown caution to the winds.

2

The fact that Christ himself would seem to have suffered not
    only the ordeal

of a cleg in the side but a midge-coronet

is enough to rattle

the best of us. The purple of Jesus's robe is so ingrained

I may find it difficult to commit, in my new version, to
    Matthew's "scarlet."

I should be able to organize a work-around

in the matter of paying off the "harlot."

There'll be no stopping the presses. That's one of the translator's
    perks.

I'll be damned if I'll allow those varlets

to confine me to barracks

like the monk who offered me matcha in the Ryoan-ji temple in
   Kyoto.

The description of Saint Paul "kicking against the pricks"

I've chosen to render as "kicking against the *goads*"

so as not to offend any shrinking violets

among the moneylenders. I'm not going to dress up "a den of
   iniquity,"

though, when it comes to the playing of skin flutes.

I'm happy to go with the flow

particularly if the story stays below the fold,

given how a warble fly

in the ointment is sometimes perceived by hoi polloi as a major
   hurdle,

as if it represents some kind of character flaw.

3

The fact that a rabble tends to rouse the rabble

is no less true of our raised bogs

than the Boulevard Saint-Germain. It's only another ripple that
   sends the ripple

across a stagnant ring over which the midges box
so clever. My horse tugs at her halter
as if they've set their beaks

at her rather than me. Even the monk illuminating my
    version of the Psalter
views this world in terms of the column inch.
I'll be damned, too, if I'll falter

before the invisible. If the idea of a garden where everything
    seems to hinge
on one of its fifteen boulders
always being hidden from view sends a shiver through my
    palfrey's haunch,

it also makes my own unease look paltry.
It's true, of course, that Saint Patrick's claim to have herded
    swine on Slemish
connects him to Saint Anthony, another consensus builder,

but the recent implanting of a microchip containing the entire
    Rhemish
Testament under the skin of my mare
confirms I'd not let a blemish

even slightly mar
my ambition. *Incorporate*, I always say, as a monk incorporates
    the hole of a warble
on a sheet of vellum into the phrase "less is m( )re."

THE FLY

Surrounded as he is by the blood spatter
from the cut and thrust over an idea to which he was but
    briefly wed,
the fly is washing his hands of the matter

till the smoke clears. A wildcatter
on a rig still lumbering across the North Sea's bed,
surrounded as he is by the blood spatter

and spout of crude, he remembers only a scatter
of crudités, heavy hors d'oeuvres, glasses, remembers seeing
    red.
The fly is washing his hands of the matter

now a meal in an upper room has once again served to shatter
his illusions. Overcome by the high hum of the dead,
surrounded as he is by the blood spatter

from the cruets of oil and vinegar, the fly is tempted to spray
    attar
of roses on the aforesaid
"fly washing his hands of the matter,"

if only because the internet chatter
points to a city about to cede to the forces of Ethelred,
surrounded as it is. By the blood spatter

you shall know them as you shall know a satyr
by its horse's ears and tail. Instead
of washing his hands of the matter,

the fly might embrace an earth that is irredeemably in tatters
(a banquet of slivers and shreds
surrounded, as it is, by the interplanetary blood spatter),

might heed the pitter-patter
of unborn fly-feet on the stair tread.
But the fly is washing his hands of the matter

even as he contemplates a platter
complete with its severed head, now the centerpiece of the
    spread.
Surrounded as he is by the blood spatter
the fly is washing his hands of the matter.

THE PANGOLIN, OR VASTY

for Paul Simon

1

It was our old friend Owen Glendower who, in *Henry IV, Part 1*,
referred to the deep as "vasty."
Each eye of each of those four bees found in a woman's eye in
    Taiwan
was made up of seven thousand or eight thousand facets.
Though we already know the human eyelash
is the scene of a mite-fest
we're still grateful to the Hubble
for introducing us to the hourglass-shaped nebula known as
    the Southern Crab.
The only living boy in the bubble
seems to have developed a tendency to smash and grab.
It's sixty years since *Freedom 7* first made a splash,
sixty years over which the nine hundred thousand pieces of
    wreckage now in orbit
have made some neighborhoods in space too risky to visit.
Only gradually will we begin to warm
to the idea that, in addition to our planet being covered in
    tosh,

we're looking at an interplanetary shit-storm

of bolts, blank discs, bling-bling,

gorgets, gewgaws, washers, wing nuts, and napkin rings.

By the end of 2020, it will seem almost irrelevant that Christo
has wrapped

the Arc de Triomphe in stuff once worn by the Yellow Vests.

2

It's stuff worn by the Yellow Vests rather than polypropylene

Christo might now harvest from a school

of right whales. Their baleen

was once recycled

for corset stays to help hourglass-shaped women cut
something of a dash.

There might be five hundred gallons of spermaceti in a single
whale skull.

While some of us are drinking doubles

in a singles bar

the only living boy in the bubble

longs for a slash to become a good old-fashioned scar.

How he admires the panache

with which those Israeli scientists used human tissue to 3D-
print a tiny heart.

On the subject of science, the King and his lackadaisical

lackeys continue to deal in bioarms

but try to quash

our conviction that climate change will result in bloodbaths
    and locust-swarms.

Authorities in Singapore recently conducted a sting

in which they thwarted the efforts of a Nigerian-Vietnamese
    smuggling ring

by intercepting two separate hoards,

each of a barely imaginable fourteen metric tons, of pangolin
    scales.

3

Those twenty-eight tons of scales were stripped from forty
    thousand so-called "anteaters"

with a view to warding off everything from dropsy (mild) to
    depression (severe),

gonorrhea, and gastroenteritis.

It's the artist's job to collect detritus and guide it back towards
    earth's atmosphere

since it's in that flash, the flash

of reentry, that something may be made clear.

In Derry and Paris they're once more picking through the
    rubble

for some outmoded cause.

The only living boy in the bubble

would seem to have developed a rash on one of his retractable
    claws.

The burn comes neither before nor after the crash.

At that moment we look behind a Taiwanese woman's eyelid

to the fact those four bees were living off her tears.

This idea that artistic froideur is the norm

is one that simply won't wash

so we'll be there when the battalions form,

standing against the King

in his pangolin-scale armor even as we make the welkin ring.

Last time we met, as I recall, you'd taken over command of the
    retrieval satellite

from our old friend, the Welsh activist Owen Glendower.

THE ICE FISHERS

The ice fishers on Bear Gulch Lake
are happy to have been left on the shelf
though each has cut a foot-thick wedding cake.

It's an unlikely form of spinsterhood
to which they're almost completely resigned.
Their poles are made of poplar wood.

They're young girls mostly, don't you know?

The ice fishers on Bear Gulch Lake
have learned what's most likely to break
the surface is some version of the self.

It's an unlikely form of spinsterhood
in which they've learned what's best withstood
the pressure is saw-toothed, three-spined—

a fish armed with a crossbow.

The ice fishers on Bear Gulch Lake
are happy to have been left on the shelf
in an unlikely form of spinsterhood
to which they're almost completely resigned.

BINGE

By carefully observing the process by which the triangle weaver
  spider
catches its prey, scientists have shown
it is the only nonhuman animal ever recorded using tools for
  power amplification.
A pensioner who was shot with a crossbow
while adjusting his satellite dish
has died almost a month later.
A Caravaggesque night scene? Painted during the Civil War?
By an Englishman? Yup.
Police are trying to identify the body of a man wearing designer
  clothes
who was found in a wheelie bin behind a Waitrose
  supermarket.
The man had a pierced ear and a mustache
and "looked like Freddie Mercury,"
according to people living nearby in Islington.
Sainsbury's was the first British supermarket chain
to sell snack-packs of insects when it introduced Eat Grub's
  crickets last year,
although they have yet to become a bestseller.
Seaweed caviar and algae milk will become popular by 2025.
And, well, I'm a slut for this kind of thing.

I want to take off my clothes and roll around in it.

At the height of her fame in the 1950s and early 1960s

Doris Day was one of the most recognizable women in the
world,

with the fatalistic song "Que Sera, Sera" her signature tune.

The mystery surrounding the deaths of a hunter and two young
women

shot dead with crossbow bolts in a Bavarian guesthouse

has deepened with the discovery of two more corpses

in a flat belonging to one of the victims.

All alone on his large farm in Nebraska, Kurt Kaser stepped on a
corn hopper.

The hopper was attached to a tube

used to raise grain from ground level for loading.

It was now sucking the sixty-three-year-old farmer footfirst

onto its churning corkscrew blade.

Mr. Kaser did the only thing he could think of:

he pulled out his three-inch pocketknife and cut off his left leg.

Steven Paul was regarded as the greatest exponent of épée
fencing of his generation.

It was Paul who doubled for Pierce Brosnan, playing James Bond,

in a celebrated fight scene in *Die Another Day* (2002).

Three Germans whose bodies were found punctured with
crossbow bolts

in a Bavarian guesthouse are thought to have decided to die
together.

The trio were avid jousters and had stopped in Passau

on the way back from a tournament in Austria.
A reference to the Little Death Club's nude, fire-eating,
    flaming nipple-tassel tosser
as "Kitty Kitty Bang Bang" was erroneous.
Miss Bang Bang is not Kitty Kitty but Kitty.
It was lovely to zone out
to the documentary *Making Waves: The Art of Cinematic Sound*,
during which I learned that in 1933 they created King Kong's
    distinctive roar
by recording a lion, slowing it down, and playing it backwards.
Ita O'Brien is a pioneer, Britain's first intimacy coordinator,
a woman who choreographs sex scenes
and teaches actors to be comfortable rolling round virtually
    naked,
apparently in the throes of ecstasy, in front of a film crew.
Three Germans killed by crossbow bolts in a bed-and-breakfast
    hotel
may have been members of a "sex-cult"
centered on a guru with a taste for medieval combat.
In proposing a statutory presumption against prosecuting
former and serving military personnel
for alleged offenses committed while serving abroad ten or
    more years ago,
Penny Mordaunt, the defense secretary, has acted judiciously.
The amnesty will not apply to misconduct in Northern Ireland.
A foul rumor is rippling through Westeros:
the final series of *Game of Thrones* isn't really very good.
The appearance of a rogue coffee cup at a feast in episode four

did little to reassure skeptics.
A body found in a wheelie bin in Islington
was that of Erik Sanfilippo, twenty-three, from Tuscany.
He was a model who loved designer clothes and was wearing
  Versace shoes.
Bones found in the mortuary chests of Winchester Cathedral
have been tentatively identified as belonging to Emma of
  Normandy.
She is the only twice-crowned Queen of England,
having married Ethelred the Unready, and then his successor,
  Canute.
It's been running for eight years and you haven't caught a
  second.
Now everybody is talking about the finale, and you're dimly
  aware
that it will be all about who ends up sitting on the Iron
  Throne
but you still don't have a clue what is going on, or for whom
  to root.
In a move that would dent Boris Johnson's chances of
  becoming leader,
Theresa May urged Tory MPs to delay a leadership election
  yesterday.
Doris Day requested no funeral, memorial service, or grave
  marker.
In *For Sama*, a full-term fetus, plucked from the womb of a
  shrapnel-shredded mother,
is presumed dead, yet suddenly coughs into life.

COW MOOSE, ROUTE 125, RIPTON, VERMONT

A throwback to 1966
what with the Vidal Sassoon bob cut fringe
trademarked by Mary Quant
and her coming into her own only at dusk
to binge

on water lilies in a sunken discotheque.
Though you may have her pegged
as a wuss, she has scant
regard for the predations of bear or coydog,
ranging out across the muskeg

to strip a dozen willow trees
of their painkilling bark and shoots.
Some nights she's got up in hot pants,
others a kind of knitted mohair minidress
set off by platform boots.

CHIPMUNK

Ain't that God's own truth?
Just one more flame-streaked roadster
fresh from the spray booth.

THE TRIUMPH

In Memory of Ciaran Carson

1

Just as a painting by Joan Miró
will stop at nothing—a mule, a bucket, a snail, a sun-bleached
    kitchen sink—
so the bone marrow

aches for more and more cancer cells. Nor would you shrink
from piling on, alas,
your tales of Captain Chemo. What we now know as the
    Westlink

began as the even less
sonorous "Belfast Urban Motorway," along which you and I
    would light out
before the Widow Douglas could sivilize

us in her own image. "*Ní fiú sin*," you'd insist, "*Ní fiú sin dada*."
We need look no further than *The Farm*,
completed in 1921–22, where Miró simply won't hesitate

from presenting the extremes
of abstraction and realism. The brainchild of Captain Terence
    O'Neill,
the Belfast Urban Motorway might have let us frame

an argument for peaceful coexistence. Now the big reveal
is we don't need British troops
to stand between us. It was the Captain's namesake you
    revered—the reels,

jigs, and hornpipes he'd transcribe
from raw recruits to the Chicago police force. "The Blackbird"
    and "Boil
the Breakfast Early." As for your trips

to the Royal Victoria Hospital, its faint aura of night soil
and Florence Nightingale, you were unbending in the face of
    the bull-roar.
Nor would you recoil

from piling on, *faraor*,
the details of your radiation treatment. That a story might
    begin "*Fadó fadó*"
was becoming increasingly rare

despite your own embodiment of our long-standing divide,
your name combining those of the Abbot of Clonmacnoise and
    a beater of the drum
for the much-vaunted Unionist veto.

2

Remember how you'd retire at nine to get a head start on your
    dreams,
dreams as vivid compared to your day-to-day as Easter is to
    ashes-and-sackcloth Lent?
There's Sir Edward Carson boarding an eastbound tram

and presenting each shipyard worker in the Queen's Island
with an autographed copy of *The Irish for No*. There's Ireland
    playing Samoa
two days after your funeral and wiping the floor with them.
    That the green linnet

will always triumph over the tooth-billed pigeon is an axiom
even the most casual reader
of Borges holds dear. There's Sir Edward again, donating a box
    of satsumas

to the leaders of the Orange Order
in Polynesia and lamenting the fact that the tradition of *sean nós*
singing doesn't begin and end with the Irish border.

And there's our old comrade-in-arms, Louis MacNeice,

peeling and portioning a mule, a bucket,

a snail, a sun-bleached kitchen sink, while the Abbot of

    Clonmacnoise

is quoting chapter and verse from your *Pocket*

Guide to Irish Traditional Music. Turlough O'Carolan based "*Sí Beag,*

    Sí Mór"

on a tune called "The Bonny Cuckoo." It's true. Not all

    Orangemen are bigots.

It's also true that, in the opening scene of *Hiroshima Mon Amour*,

we're presented not with a love-twitch but a death-twitch

of human limbs. The use of the word "mere"

to describe the Irish comes from the Latin *merus*, meaning

    "pure." The cuckoo will hatch

a plot along with any straight-up gombeen

man from the DUP who's hoping to gain even the slightest

    advantage

over your ordinary gobshite. With regard to countering the

    1956–62 Border Campaign,

Captain Francis O'Neill recommends that a force

comprised mainly of flute players, each armed with a *camán*,

should do the trick. Were they to compose in the sequence of
    the musical phrase,
like Ezra Pound or Christy Ring,
they'll likely happen on the single point that includes every
    other point in the universe.

3

Back in the day when our political representatives at least
    showed up at the Althing
you drove my Triumph Herald convertible from Notting Hill to
    the Beeb
to buy cigarettes from a vending machine. The car roof
    flapped like the wing

of some bird of death as we passed the shuttered shops and
    pubs
of Bradbury Place and Shaftesbury Square, yet we followed
    Clare's Dragoons
to the accompaniment of jigs, reels, and hornpipes

played by Nollaig and Arty, and ballads sung by Len and
    Pádraigín.
It was 2:00 a.m. Hard to reconcile *Anois teacht an Earraigh*
with the landscape of 1970s Belfast, or the landscape of
    Tarragona

with its invasive eucalyptus. Now we were composing hymns
    to the nightjar

that alerted the populace to the 836 Viking attack on Santry,
to the arctic char

that colonized Irish lakes about eighteen thousand years ago.
    The bombed-out city center
was plastered with Business as Usual signs despite the "rash"
of car bombs and incendiary

devices smoldering after the red rush
of Monaghan and La Mon.
Aunt Polly still had a bee in her bonnet about our each taking
    a whitewash brush

to the fence that ran between the Ulster Unionists and the
    main
opposition parties but we were more interested in whether a
    witchetty grub
really does taste of almonds or if *muin*

is indeed the eleventh letter of the ogham alphabet. An island
    on Lough Corrib
has a standing stone of Silurian grit (*Quel drag!*)
on which the ogham has been scrubbed

and replaced with Latin by the first in a succession of native
    monks who'd have no truck
with their native culture.
It took Miró eighteen months, moving between Mont-roig

and Montmartre, to so clearly get down the clutter

of *The Farm*, painting and repainting the watering can, the wagon,
the half-ruin

of a barn full of blunt instruments, the plow with its incisive
coulter.

4

Just as O'Carolan was influenced by Vivaldi so our trademark
    trí rainn agus amhrán
owes something to the Italian sonnet. We were determined to
    misspend
our old age in constant reruns

of our conversations on Alain Resnais having no interest in
    beginnings or ends
and our own eschewal of the conventional story line
as we tied up to a towhead in a big bend

on the Illinois side of the Lagan round about the time Resnais
    won the Golden Lion
for *Last Year at Marienbad*. Now they're saying psychedelics
may have some positive impact. Aunt Polly wanted us to
    whitewash the Peace Line

but you, being an all-round wise guy, *fear glic*,
smart aleck, and fly boy,
were willing to enter into dialogue

with the gobshites in the Althing only if they erected a statue
    not to Henry Joy
but Mary Ann McCracken. It was because I was again the worse
    for wear you'd driven
the Triumph Herald from Notting Hill by way of Illinois,

Dante's Ravenna, and the Tropical Ravine
in which Ireland would later train for the Samoa match, all the
    while guided by the reek
of a cigarette machine. The roof flapped like the wing of a raven

wheeling above the Law Rock
from which you now held forth on the comparative merits of
    Faraday's or Kinsella's *Táin*
or how "The Rakes

of Mallow" was first known as "The Rigs of Marlow," or why the
    coronation stone
that had been relocated from Tara to Scotland could be heard to
    wail
when a false king rode by. You loved nothing more than a
    couple of tunes

with Deirdre in Pat's or the Rotterdam. *Feách anois me lem aghaidh
    ar Bhalla.*
Antoine O'Reachtaire, of course, must still haunt
the road from Claremorris to Castlebar as does Willie

Clancy the road from Spanish Point to Miltown Malbay. You
were always ready to hand
down a judgment on how Willie's fingering was influenced by
Garret Barry's.
Gearóid de Barra. Born in 1847. Blind. Loved a tipple. Hint
hint.

5

It seems less odd, in retrospect, that you did so much of your
    best work in prose
given your fascination with how the osteoblast
is bent on building bone. Isn't it odd that the term "peruse"

may suggest both a close reading and a cursory? The idea
    implicit
in "The Aleph"
is that the first letter of the Hebrew alphabet is a return to a
    long list

of shibboleths
meant to trip you up. A reed
instrument is not to be confused with a flute. Rather than
    ashes and sackcloth,

you wore such a riot
of color you were a dyed-in-the-wool Mr. Natty.
You could easily have built a full-scale replica of Carrick-a-Rede

from your collection of neckwear, each tied in a Windsor
    knot,
not to speak of your top-heaviness in hats.
I think of you standing on the threshold of the Cancer Unit

at the City Hospital, still in the height
of fashion, like Walter Sickert
standing on the cusp between Impressionism and Modernism.
    The horse's head

through which I used to speak wasn't part of some
    masquerade
but represented who I truly was. And it wasn't the cat that got
    your tongue,
of course, but the cigarettes

for the love of which you'd driven my rinky-dink
Triumph Herald to the Beeb. It was a plan about which you'd
    been initially hesitant
since you knew nothing about driving. However, the dunnock

that appears in "The More a Man Has the More a Man Wants"
knows nothing about bread and cheese. That's the
    yellowhammer. Quite separate.
Despite his mild speech impediment,

Saint Ciaran of Clonmacnoise would insist that his bones be
     spread
on the hillside for the benefit of the scald crow, the badger, the
     satchel-gnawing fox,
so that he would live on not in splinters but in his whole spirit.

6

Garret Barry was most likely a victim of smallpox,
along with Donnacha Caoch and Séamus Dall. That moment
    when Turnbull's face
is indivisible from the face of Turnbull's horse always knocks

me for six between the popping crease and the square leg.
    Though our literary views
were based almost exclusively on the tradition of Prac. Crit.
as smoked by I. A. Richards and F. R. Leavis

(whom we heard lecture in the Whitla Hall), we knew that
    Corkery and Mac Cuarta
might yet make common cause
with Calvino and Kundera. Along with your collections of
    stamps and postcards

might have been a collection of tchotchkes
from the shipyard. There's Sir Edward again, distributing copies
    of *Last Night's Fun*
to a populace pretty much inured to water cannons and tear gas

never mind the paver-baps from Barney Hughes's Bakery Van.
We must already have spent the evening in the Club Bar or
    the Eg or the Bot
in contemplation of the Irishness of Huck Finn,

whether "huckleberry" might translate as *fraochán*, whether
    Last Year at Marienbad
was a kind of own goal,
whether soccer was a foreign game, whether sessions in the
    Rotterdam or Pat's

were likely to include more tunes from Sligo than Donegal,
whether it was even remotely possible that "The Rakes of
    Mallow"
was repurposed by Muthuswami Dikshitar as a hymn to
    Minakshi, whether Inchagoill

is the only site on which ogham has been purged, whether his
    interjection "Lo!"
is of a piece with Ezra
Pound's "make it new," whether the line "when lovely woman
    stooped so low"

might combine Goldsmith and "Gathering Mushrooms,"
    whether St. Louis, Missouri,
might really be the basis of a brief flashback
in "The Dry Salvages," whether an ossuary

is a plausible final resting place of the fairy folk in "*Sí Beag,*
Sí Mór," whether "Boil the Beefsteak Early" and "Boil the
   Breakfast Early"
are the same tune, whether a fox might indeed have gnawed
   your father's postal bag.

7

Just as Séamus Dall Mac Cuarta would look far beyond the
    kingdom of Oriel
to verse "that hath in it some pith"
so you would look beyond the wedding arch of hurleys

held up by an elite band of Ostmen and osteopaths
you had met in the Valley
of the False Kings to a wide-ranging discussion of the Brehon
    Laws on the beehive,

of Cootehill and Clones as the preferable venue for either the
    Ulster Fleadh
or Fleadh Cheoil na hÉireann
(a crowd pressing in to record a version of "Johnny Doherty's
    Reel"), of Fintan Vallely

having it over Séamus Tansey on the flute, of the quatrain
beloved of Séamus Dall being in essence a couplet on steroids,
    faith and begorrah,
of whether it would strain

credibility, might indeed beggar

belief, to suggest "*An Lon Dubh Báite*" derived, *i measc*

rudaí eile, from "Phyllyp Sparowe." Arty had played with Brian
   Coll and the Buckaroos

for so many years your *Pocket Guide to Irish Traditional Music*

should have featured the electric guitar, no? Along with riot
   shields, batons,

rubber bullets, and gas masks,

Captain O'Neill still recommends an auxiliary force of button

accordionists to augment the flute

players already signed up to put down the Border Campaign.
   Can it be that wood betony

is proof against fluid

on the lungs, as proposed by Nicholas Culpeper?

In 1974, the year of the firebombing of your beloved market in
   Smithfield,

we tried to translate "*An Lon Dubh Báite*," Seamus Dall's mock-
   heroic tear-gulper

about a bird belonging to an O'Neill princess that's perished

in a pail of whitewash. The innards of the zampogna, the
   bagpipes of Calabria,

are as convoluted as the innards of a Peugeot pepper mill. As
    for the Cambridge
priests familiar to John Skelton, there was not one whit
of difference between them and the twit-boy by whom the
    Inchagoill stone was purged.

8

Your time at the Arts Council was a bit like Graham Greene's
    at Eyre & Spottiswoode
or Russell Hoban's
at J. Walter Thompson, only with even greater dingbats and
    dimwits

at the helm. The big question was if the single malts of Oban
had it over the single malts of Islay or if Skelton himself was a
    smoking coach in the train
that went back to Catullus and Lesbia's own pet dunnock.
    When Michael Open

introduced us to Buñuel at the Queen's Film Theatre we
    recognized the terrain
of *That Obscure Object of Desire*
with its two actors sharing a single role just as, in the
    Triumph, you would turn

the steering wheel while I somehow worked the clutch and
    shifted gears. An Irish friar
who taught John Skelton

may also have influenced the rhyme scheme of "Phyllyp
     Sparowe." A command wire

is connected not only to six sticks of blasting gelatin
with its distinctive smell of witchetty grubs but to the entire
     network of blowhards
ranging from Saint Paul's uncircumcised Galatians

to Captain O'Neill and his Anatolian bagpipers. So it was that
     Nollaig and Arty
would guide us through a rabbit warren by way of a dovecote
to the bypassed heart

of Belfast. So it was that Len and Pádraigín would guide
us on our cigarette-safari
in the Triumph Herald already loaded with all kinds of grave
     goods—

the mule, the bucket, the snail, the right forearm of Saint
     Francis Xavier
with which proceedings might be brought to a halt
at any moment. There's Sir Edward again, urging his people to
     persevere

in the belief that to have is to have to hold.
The fact you've now been squeezed
into a columbarium in Saint Patrick's might be the first time
     you've been pigeonholed.

As we started along the Westlink on our vision-quest
we remembered that crowd pressing in to record a version of
     "Johnny Doherty's Reel"
in the square at Clones only to discover they were listening to
     a cassette.

9

The cassette tape and cassette player are things of the past,
    along with the rhyme royal
Skelton used, in *Magnificence*, to indicate a gombeen man
    putting one over
on a gobshite. But there's Sir Edward again, again ready to rail

against all those who might favor
a false king, one with the slightest blemish. Your own mien
is flawless, your trilby set off with a feather

as you stand on the threshold of the Cancer Unit. Isn't it odd
    that the term "moan"
may suggest both pain and pleasure? Hell slap
it into them, right? We who were so keen to undermine

all authority would come to legislate on whether that was a
    "light" jig or a "slip"
played by Michael Coleman and Deirdre,
on whether a syllabub

is essentially a posset, on whether Strabo merely followed
    Diodorus
in deeming us cannibals, on what Buñuel's take on O'Grady's
    take on *The Colloquy*
with the Ancients might have been. The Territory

for which you and I were lighting out was one where Gaelic
and Esperanto were the official languages. I continue to work
    the clutch and shift gears
and you, *an fear níos glice,*

continue to steer between the square leg umpire and the
    umpire at the popping crease.
Doomed as we are to paint and repaint
the watering can, the wagon, the plow, so an enfant terrible
    becomes an éminence grise

and Aunt Polly is destined to forever have a bee in her bonnet
about your faking your death with blood from that piglet in
    the pram.
As for the Aleph, the single point in the universe that includes
    every other point,

that's surely the columbarium
in which your ashes lie, where "The Bonny Cuckoo" and
    Donnacha Caoch
melt into the fact that MacNeice's "Snow" is set in Brum

and the fact *The Annals of Ulster* make no mention of the
earthquake
of 1508, that being almost certainly the year in which Skelton
wrote "Phyllyp Sparowe."
It was in 1509, you're pretty sure, that Art O'Neill was
crowned at Tullyhogue.

SALONICA

That young woman's body sprawled by the side of the road
looked as if it had been thrown clear
like a burden her car desperately needed to off-load.
The car itself was pretty much a write-off,
a cairn of chrome and windshield glass
dating back to the Romans or, at least, the Romanovs.
As she flew through the air
her dress must have ridden halfway up her back,
leaving her buttocks bare.
Another driver had come to a stop
and was already on the phone
with the emergency services or the cops.
I very much doubt we'd have been of the slightest help
had we pulled over on our way to the airport
to give her—what?—a howdie-skelp.
In the days when we still welcomed someone into the world
we wouldn't have thought it strange
that a collet be lightly knurled.
In the Archaeological Museum there's at least one artifact
for which the use is no longer known.
We approach it, therefore, with a modicum of tact.
That young woman's body sprawled by the side of the road
represented yet another episode

around which we would do our best to steer.

Another driver had come to a stop

and was picking his way over the predawn blacktop

to where she lay three-quarters prone.

I very much doubt we'd have been of the slightest help.

If the ambulance we'd meet could barely manage a yelp

anything we might have done would have been a falling short.

As she flew through the air

after her car had hit a pole she may have felt a pang of despair

to think her grasp on things had now gone slack.

The car itself was pretty much a write-off.

Be it a circlet for a coif

or a hoop through which a soul might pass

in the days when we still welcomed someone into the world,

or a ferrule from a javelin hurled

beyond our range,

in the Archaeological Museum there's at least one artifact

from a past we simply cannot reenact.

It may be ivory. It may be deer-bone.

That young woman's body sprawled by the side of the road

looked as if it had been thrown clear.

As she flew through the air

her skirt had ridden halfway up her back.

The car itself was pretty much a write-off,

a cairn of chrome and windshield glass.

Another driver had come to a stop

and was already on the phone

so I very much doubt we'd have been of the slightest help
had we pulled over on our way to the airport.
In the days when we still welcomed someone into the world
we wouldn't have thought it strange
in the Archaeological Museum there's at least one artifact
for which the use is no longer known.

THE BANISTERS

Our ornamental gates and railings that were melted down
for rifle barrels have gained some sort of posthumous renown

by unambiguously drawing a line in the sand.
The gates and railings are finally taking a firm stand

and even more emphatically bringing things to a close.
The exit wound is their approximation of a rose

or a geranium under gauze on the windowsill.
Gangrene. The green and gold of the first full-blown daffodil.

Also rendered, so it would even more tellingly rend,
was lead stripped from the gutters and flashing. For lead will
    bend

along a spine as it did along a walnut ridge post.
What was once an outer sanctum is now the innermost.

Shouldered as rifle stocks, after a mere three weeks of drill,
the banisters are gradually taking another hill.

THE SHEET

We were sitting in a village square
not so very much broader than the bridal suite
that overlooked it,
the suite where we'd spent at least part of that afternoon

extending our modest repertoire
of love-forays and love-feats.
Now we made do with playing footsie
at a café table

while pondering fettucine with sage. *Plein air* or *en plein air*?
You checked your iPhone. A culinary herb,
native to southern Europe
and the Mediterranean,

once thought to grow best
in households where the wife is dominant.
Even though the supporting evidence was far from scant,
this was a theory I must put to rest,

given the frantic smoothing out of air
by the man and two young boys hoisting a sheet
through what was irreparably twilight.
A grandfather and, you surmised, his two grandsons

were about to run a test
on the projector that had only recently become a prominent
feature of our lives. It looked very much as if the eggplant
was introduced to the West

by Alexander the Great. As to whether normal wear and tear
could have accounted for the rip
in your Himalayan wrap
(itself a shade of aubergine

in a blend of wool and moire),
the jury was still out.
Acquainted though we'd been with the fact cellulose nitrate
is notoriously unstable,

we were nonetheless taken unawares
when the reel of film began to disintegrate
even as images of what looked like some of our earlier exploits
were thrown up on the screen.

LE JONGLEUR

Some days it looks as if I might be limbering up
for my role as a human cannonball
complete with an athletic cup.
When it comes to protecting my thingamajig
I take my cue from the Good Thief
and stay close to Mr. Big.
Mr. Big always gave it his best shot
for those few years he found himself in the ring
and managed to get out of some pretty tight spots.
Often I'm simply going through the hoops
of practicing the Chinese pole
while the ring is cleared of elephant poop.
For I may unabashedly fly the flag
of the newly independent country of myself
while working on a new car gag,
the one in which I put my trust
in the removal of all sagging springs.
Some bring back the tusks of an elephant in must.
Most afternoons I find myself plying three Indian clubs
as I wait in the cloud-gray vestibule
for a smack in the gub
from the big top's sawdust- and tiger-fug
by which I'm still more often than not revived.

Each elephant sports its own hessian rug.
Some days it looks as if I might be limbering up
while the elephants go huppity-hup
through Uttar Pradesh or the Transvaal.
When it comes to protecting my thingamajig
I couldn't give a fig
about wearing a fig leaf.
Mr. Big always gave it his best shot
but even he ended up hanging by his topknot
like one of those acrobats from Beijing.
Often I'm simply going through the hoops
rather than actually looping the loop
with Diavalo at Barnum's or the brothers Cole.
Or I may unabashedly fly the flag
for Mr. Big or the Good Thief or any of the ragtag
pickled punks they keep on the top shelf.
The one in which I put my trust
is the motorcar that's built of rust
and spit and cardboard and bloody butcher's string.
Most afternoons I find myself plying three Indian clubs
while the world shrinks to the size of an upturned tub
for an elephant who's learned to abide by the rules
of the big top's sawdust- and tiger-fug.
To get nineteen clowns *into* a Volkswagen Bug
requires the ministrations of at least three midwives.
Some days it looks as if I might be limbering up
for my role as a human cannonball.

When it comes to protecting my thingamajig
I take my cue from the Good Thief.
Mr. Big always gave it his best shot
for those few years he found himself in the ring.
Often I'm simply going through the hoops
of practicing the Chinese pole
so I may unabashedly fly the flag
of the newly independent country of myself,
the one in which I put my trust
in the removal of all sagging springs.
Most afternoons I find myself plying three Indian clubs
as I wait in the cloud-gray vestibule
for the big top's sawdust- and tiger-fug
by which I'm still more often than not revived.

AN ITEM

Again I found myself at a party in that big-windowed room
overlooking a kitchen midden
alongside my wife and a woman with whom

I'd once been smitten.
I'd remembered her as Faith. Now she went by Hope.
"'Lovely Rita,'" Hope was saying, "is a semitone

higher because the tape was speeded up."
"Aren't we just a little too far inland to be eating steamers?"
"There's a case for calling a prenup a *post*nup."

"It's the same root. To stem. To stammer."
"They're both Anabaptist sects. It goes back to some schism."
"Our biggest problem is we're no longer customers

viewing the world through the prism
of the mine or the steel mill. This is an entirely new mode
of postindustrial capitalism

in which we ourselves are the commodity."
It was with a sense of déjà-vu we watched the livestream
from beyond the meadow

of that Amish plowman who'd stopped unpicking a furrow-seam
to realign the harness pads, collars, and hames
on his three-abreast team.

OSCAR WILDE AT THE PAVILION HOTEL

As he holds forth on the subject of "The Decorative Arts"
the smell of Brimstone Creek
conveys him to that realm of *le désespoir*
in which the flesh is willing but the spirit weak.
Since he waltzed off the ship
in January, this trip
has already seen him lounging in so many far-flung parts
to offer his critique

of "that which hallows the vessels
of everyday use," the very horsehair couch
now longs to be released
from the burden of its being. He won't quite vouch
for his own being in the grip
of a rose-hipped
angel in the front row who seems to overly wrestle
with his meaning, yet Oscar senses they might yet crouch

in a river-fault
overwhelmed by the same purple loosestrife
as stowed away in the *Arizona*'s ballast.
A deckhand has been known to find beauty in a butter knife

and a hulking Chinese navvy to sip
tea from a bone china lip.
Back in London, all the while, a pillar of salt
is turning into the woman who'll shortly become his wife.

VIRAL

1

Any one of these masked avengers
might be moonlighting as another Captain Rock,
might set out not only to censure
but incinerate a rich farmer dreading his knock

at midnight, a cowpuncher, a calf-drencher,
a dweeb journalist, a helmetless jock
courting death by misadventure,
a negotiator trying to break the deadlock

between boss and union, a prominent backbencher
imagining he's standing for reelection
when he's making a speech from the dock,

a career civil servant both inured and indentured
to a twice daily intravenous injection
of horse piss and poppycock.

2

Any one of them might be an insurance underwriter
taking the tube from Maida Vale,
an architect pulling an all-nighter
while she works to scale,

a private investigator flicking a cigarette lighter
and putting another nail
in his coffin, a developer of an antibody titer,
a Muddy Waters failing to curtail

a Lightnin' Hopkins, a bishop adjusting his miter,
a baker proffering a baker's dozen
of cakes and ale,

a professional flautist, an amateur firefighter,
a migrant worker who met your forty-second cousin
at the blading of the kale.

3

Any one of these masked avengers
might be moonlighting as Atticus Finch,
might be reliant on the kindness of strangers,
a blue man of the Minch

crossed with a ginger, a money exchanger
feeling the pinch,
a lumberjack, a barista, a Texas Ranger
tightening the cinch

on any one of these masked avengers
moonlighting as a butterfly nun, a lab technician,
a boxer prolonging a clinch

rather than putting themself in danger,
a restorer of Tintoretto or Titian
taking on the world square inch by square inch.

A BULL

Every day putting a fresh spin
on how he maintains that shit-eating grin
despite his notoriously thin skin.
The quagmire of what-might-have-been.

Every day shouldering an invisible tray.
Hello, hello. Olé, Olé.
His musing on how best to waylay
a hiker passing through a field of Galloways.

Every day aiming to swat
the single fly that keeps tying and untying a knot
before taking another potshot.
Rolling through the Krishna Valley like a juggernaut.

Every day trying to err
on the side of standing firm. Foursquare.
The singlemindedness of a Berber
about to take out a French Legionnaire.

Every day getting through by dint
of three of his four hooves being knapped flint.
Hanging out the bloody bandage of his, hint hint,
barber's pole. His stick of peppermint.

Every day his hoofprints in the sand-strewn park
have enclosed so much in quotation marks.
Not even Job or Abraham, hark hark,
is a patch on our patriarch.

Every day the holy show
of leather dyed robin's-egg blue by Tiffany & Co.
Areas strictly off-limits? Strictly no-go?
The wilds of Connaught. The stockyards of Chicago.

Every day rising at 5:00 a.m.,
determined to stem
the flow of misinformation from the well at Zem-Zem.
His dangle-straw from a crib in Bethlehem.

Every day fighting shy
of the possibility his eye
is a shellac-gouge from an old hi-fi.
His helmet appropriated from a samurai.

Every day the mob
threatening a hatchet job.
Their hobbling across concrete. Hobnob. Hobnob.
Their sidelong glances at his thingmabob.

Every day the urge to rut
at odds with his yen for whole grain calf nuts.
The "my-my" and "tut-tut"
of that bevy of cattle at their scuttlebutt.

Every day his own cow's lick
even more at odds with his almighty mick.
How come his second cousin, the dik-dik,
gets to trip the light fantastic?

Every day taking a bow
before settling back to plow
the rowdy-dow-dow
of a Filipino swamp buffalo, or carabao.

Every day plotting how to get even even with the get
who's trolling him on the internet.
Under the vapor trails of the jet set
the solidity of his silhouette.

Every day his image picked out in tin
to signify there being room at the Inn.
Bottoms up. Chin-chin.
The gulping of milk punch from a pannikin.

Every day cruising the main drag
in anticipation of raising his own red flag
to the plaza's ragtag
bunch of scamps and scallywags.

Every day forced to cram
for some big exam.
The difference between *quondam* and *quamdam*.
The origins of the dithyramb.

Every day a razor. Every night a strop.
Rush tickets for *Carmen* at the Met cost twenty-five dollars a pop.
Get a move on, would you? Chop chop.
A world in which so much "art" is agitprop.

Every day taking a hit
from some little shit
armed with the latest version of lit crit.
The fly still looping the loop in his Messerschmitt.

Every day, it would seem, rekindling a flame
against the culture of shame
and its interminable blame game.
Every day countering a counterclaim.

Every day forced to pit
himself against Holy Writ
and the nitwit
for whom the Lascaux paintings are counterfeit.

Every day having to whisk
away the versifiers averse to risk.
The ignominy of being supplanted, tsk tsk,
by a ram on an Egyptian obelisk.

Every day lying down with the lamb.
What-might-have-been? More water over the dam.
Having to meet the future head-on. Wham-bam.
His muzzle a spermicide-slick diaphragm.

Every day the thrill
of balancing a natural proclivity and an acquired skill
after a walk-on part in *Cattle Drive* with Chill Wills.
His tongue turquoise-teal from chlorophyll.

Every day learning not to pin
his hopes on there being grain in the bin.
The situation supposedly win-win
when he mounts an upholstered Holstein mannikin.

Every day the likelihood of a snub
from a warble grub
even as he rises above the hubbub.
Every day the flash-freezing of his syllabub.

Every day busting sod
whilst straddling a divining rod.
His permanent disdain for the god squad
by whom he was once overawed.

Every day contending with the holier-than-thou
attitude associated with the sacred cow,
"kowtow" and "powwow"
being terms he's now obliged to disavow.

Every day cutting some slack
to the youths leaping over his back
in Knossos. His dream of trading endless ack-ack
for a week on the Concord and Merrimack.

Every day starting to dig
with his one obsidian hoof through the rigs.
A lily pad where a bigwig
flies in and out in some sort of whirligig.

Every day muddling through
thanks to his tried and true
ability to rise above the general to-do
by thinking of it all as déjà-vu.

Every day chewing gum
like a teddy boy in a bombed-out slum.
As for his success in rising above the humdrum?
For a moment only. Only a modicum.

Every day striking a blow
against a more-or-less invisible foe.
A life lived in slo-mo
ever since a chute opened at the rodeo.

Every day creating a stink
against being pushed to the brink
by the powers that be (nod nod, wink wink)
with their newspeak and doublethink.

Every day those massive chords on the synth
as he's rabble-roused from his plinth.
His taking everything to the nth
degree despite being consigned to a labyrinth.

Every livelong
day making of his hide a parish-encircling thong.
His panko-encrusted balls a delicacy in Hong Kong.
Subsisting on a diet of mashed kurrajong.

Every day waiting for someone to deign
to give him free rein.
That shit-eating grin. How's it maintained?
Running rings around a mill that crushes sugarcane.

Every day trying to weigh
in the scales those who still flay
the burnt offering and those who nay-say
such exaltation of the everyday.

Every day making a dry run
for either his moment in the sun
or an air-injection captive bolt stun gun.
The china shop of his skeleton.

PLAGUEY HILL

1

At the end of our driveway, the yellow recycling bin
will be picked up this morning by Vlad,
our Superintendent of Public Works. I certainly don't want to
    impugn
the motives of the village elders who, after the big flood

washed it out, closed our road to through traffic.
That's proved to be largely a godsend;
it's now only once or twice a day an Orphic
figure passes, glancing back for whatever has his scent

and will, somewhat soonish, tear him limb from limb.
Were it open, the picture house in Cobleskill
would be showing a shoot 'em up or creature feature.

For three weeks now, Jean and I have been on the lam
in Sharon Springs, a couple of old-school
bank robbers lying low for the foreseeable future.

2

It's not so long ago the future
held out the promise of travel to another antique land
unknown as yet to Frommer or Fodor.
I spent yesterday ignorant of the fact the valiant

Adam Schlesinger has gone the way of all dust.
Together with Chris Collingwood, Adam made Fountains of
    Wayne
a band whose songs combined the height of literary taste
with low-blow hooks. Ai Fen, a doctor from Wuhan

who blew the whistle on the Chinese Politburo
seems to have been "disappeared" by those sons of bitches.
No motion hath she now? As for our homegrown kingpin,

he's warning us against narcos on burros.
The Pentagon has ordered 100,000 "Human Remains Pouches."
Once we subscribed to the idea of boxes made of pine.

3

We've subscribed to the idea of boxes made of maple or pine
since the first American Civil War,
when mass production of caskets offered a kind of boon
and the funeral parlor a conversation piece. The Army Corps

of Engineers is preparing for the worst.
There's a very fine line between the enforcement of a
    lockdown
and good old-fashioned house arrest.
There's hardly an election

that isn't rigged, hardly an institution not in ruins.
With the power of the European
Union seriously under threat, Hungarian "voters"

have given free rein
to Prime Minister Viktor Orbán,
who knows only too well the people make perfect cannon
    fodder.

4

In Ireland, the use of straw for cattle fodder
may be ruled out by a particularly wet summer. I'm thinking
    777
and the resulting murrain. What with our theaters
being dark and the national tour of *Dear Evan*

Hansen in abeyance, Asher is back on the Upper
West Side and working on his new musical about Burke and
    Hare.

In 1832, there was a widespread belief that straw-tapers
or straw-spills might dispel cholera from the Irish air.

Yesterday, Jean took a ballet class by Zoom,
improvising a barre on the banisters.
What to watch tonight? Some will lament

my already lowering the bar to take in *High Lonesome*
and *High Noon*; maybe the exploits of the Starks and Lannisters
are also a topic of interest to the serious mind?

5

A genuine topic of interest to the serious mind
is the firing of Captain Crozier of the USS *Theodore Roosevelt*
for expressing concern for those under his command.
Nearly 10 million Americans have filed

for unemployment in the last two weeks.
The firing of Captain Crozier will be a defining moment of
    this episode
when the names of the bigwigs
in the West Wing are forgotten. Murrain, or rinderpest,

is characterized by fever, dysentery, a nasal discharge.
Dorothy and Ryan are today donning their masks

and driving to South Salem. They were meant to be married in
    the fall

in that same pine grove Jean and I took for church.
As a child, Dorothy couldn't distinguish between "mucus" and
    "music."
Some cattle present one or two symptoms. Some present all.

6

I'm not sure if Governor Cuomo's shipment of one thousand
    ventilators are all
present and accounted for;
I do know it took two Chinese billionaires to breach the Great
    Wall
and somehow spirit them to New York. There's a fair

chance these next few days will see the city's death toll peak.
At least one of those billionaires, Joe Tsai, owns both the
    Brooklyn Nets
and the Barclays Center, where we'd managed to book
tickets for Elton John this "Alright for Fighting" Saturday
    night.

Last evening I broiled the sable
that had been delivered by FedEx. It's my way of flying the
    coop.
There has to be an upside to being largely housebound

and, though it was farm-raised, that sable
met all expectations. As for those nineteen thousand fans,
    their mouths agape,
when I think of them I think of a burial mound.

7

The Gaelic term *tamhlacht* refers specifically to a burial mound
for victims of bubonic plague.
One of my heroes, Robert Graves, came to believe the Maenads
would get totally blocked

not on booze but fly agaric. I'm on leave this semester
but today must read applications for How to Write a Sonnet,
a course I'll teach in the fall. Those who pass muster
will find themselves glancing back at whatever has their scent

and will, somewhat soonish, tear them limb from limb.
Another hero, Dionysius the Areopagite, won't force me to
    choose
between my devotion to Times Square and my umbilical

attachment to Tamlaght and Tamnamore. The light from the
    lamps
is interpenetrating, yet distinct. I'm pretty sure P. W. Joyce
renders Tamnamore as "the great plague hill."

8

Today's the day our Superintendent of Public Works comes
    down the hill
to pick up both our recycling and our trash.
I turn from the Christian iconography of *The Outlaw Josey Wales*
to offer a running commentary, a little midrash,

on living off the cuff.
I've not made much of it, since I don't want to be seen to
    garner
attention, but after two weeks of a dry cough
and general aches and pains, I now seem to have turned a
    corner.

The fact that Gethsemane translates to "olive press"
gives another layer of significance to Christ's sweating drops
    of blood.
He knows in his bones he's about to foist

himself on an unsuspecting public. Bernard Murtagh didn't
    brace
himself since he didn't know he was about to further a plot.
It seems Bernard Murtagh was the first known victim of
    cholera in Belfast.

9

What Friar's Bush graveyard stands for in Belfast
is a cholera pit from 1832 and, from 1847, a famine pit.
This second night of Passover we'll feast
on chicken and green beans. Next week I'll add soil to the
    raised beds

in which I grow the herbs that, dried, so enliven
pasta sauce and scrambled eggs. Mary Powers and my sister,
    Maureen,
shared an anniversary last Saturday. Dear Michael Heffernan
would have been seventy-three tomorrow. A "grievous
    murrain"

was the fifth plague to strike Egypt. Our family seder
will be conducted by Zoom. Those allowed to move about after
    curfew
in the Vilna ghetto must show a certificate. Shopping for
    victuals

is akin to choosing a suitor
whilst ripping out what you've woven through the day. The
    mass grave
is a meadow filled with asphodels.

10

For it's not to Elysian fields but those meadows filled with
    asphodels
the run-of-the-mill dead are consigned in Homer.
Over the last month, Jean and I have developed such a fatal
addiction to *Boardwalk Empire*

we've watched all five seasons on the trot. Good Friday sees
    snow
across the Mohawk Valley to the Adirondacks.
A passage from the Book of Enoch lays a sinew
on the concept of the "Son of Man." John Wayne, in his dog
    tags,

is pointing yet again to the wreath
of thorns on the Redeemer of the Andes.
It occurred to me only today that "lucifer" is a version of
    "phosphorus."

The lesser celandine so beloved of Wordsworth
is an invasive species. Knotweed, too. Its scourge of knots.
As Chile had given Ireland fuchsia so Ireland would give Chile
    furze.

11

There's a fire backlighting the word "furze,"
the fire long thought to be crucial to its renewal.
The 2014 dictionary of the Royal Spanish Academy lists
    "avarice"
as a characteristic of the Jew. To slip in "diurnal"

is one of Wordsworth's boldest moves, as *la soupe de lentilles*
is a jazzed-up "mess of pottage." A mezuzah
is required for any room with two doorposts and a lintel.
Still no word on Ai Fen. I miss. You miss. She misses.

The message attached by a canister to the leg of a pigeon?
Continue to hold your hands for as long
as twenty seconds under the hot water faucet.

"The virus has but one ambition,"
says a sickle-bearing Doctor Fauci, "and that's getting into our
    lungs.
To that end it's working hand over fist."

12

In New York they've been working hand over fist
to bury the dead stored in upwards of fifty refrigerated trucks.

Though yesterday saw more snow on the ground I was keen to invest

in dyeing eggs for this morning. I'd forgotten that Dirk

Bogarde was among the first into Belsen when the stone
was rolled away. The character of Tadzio is based on one of those Polish barons
one meets in Venice. When I was a boy, our eggs were stained
with furze blossom or, as here, the Earl Grey tea I use for steeping prunes.

In 1823, two men were apprehended at Belfast docks with the bodies
of a woman and child recently buried in Friar's Bush
now packed in sawdust in a barrel. As a person ages, the occipital

bone fuses with the other bones in the cranium. Jean and I put on our boots
and roll our eggs downhill till their skulls are bashed.
Those two bodies were most likely in transit to a Scottish teaching hospital.

One of our village elders, Doug, is undergoing chemo at the
   hospital
in Cooperstown. In my effort to be a better person I'll drop off
   a little tiffin
for his husband, Garth. As for those lickspittles
in Samaritan's Purse, I'm glad the Cathedral of Saint John the
   Divine

called them out as anti-LGBT bigots and won't give them
   houseroom.
It used to be the clergy railed only about the dangers of
   crossroad dance halls.
In ponying up $10 million, Bono and U2 may help us develop
   our own truth serum.
My colleague Paul Lansky's "Table's Clear" is played on
   kitchen utensils.

At seven o'clock each evening we serenade with pots and pans
   the forgotten
now classed as "essential." People who get their hands dirty.
The incessant hand washing practiced by the Pharisees

was enough to give Christ kittens.
Our kingpin is himself recognized as being not only tawdry
   but negligently tardy
in making preparations to treat the victims of coronavirus.

14

The previously unclaimed bodies of the victims of coronavirus
buried in the potter's field
of Hart Island must now be claimed by all of us. We must each
    be an Orpheus,
compulsively checking our facts. I'll write a thank-you note to
    Vlad

and leave him a little care package. Seesawed. The market has
    seesawed.
Who knew asphodel leaves stay fresh for exactly as long as
    burrata?
My calendar is a palimpsest
in which what might have been ghosts what's actually
    transpired.

Tonight our band, Rogue Oliphant, was meant to play Joe's
    Pub;
the show's rescheduled for next February. It's poems spoken
    not by Balaam
but Balaam's ass I want to write. Their predilection for
    henbane

no less than fly agaric lay behind the Maenads' weakness for
    shoot 'em ups
and creature features. I myself need look no further for an
    emblem
than the end of the driveway and that recycling bin.

15

At the end of our driveway, a standard yellow recycling bin
brings back the idea of a future
to which we once subscribed. Even as I pine
for a past in which the use of straw for cattle fodder

was a topic of interest to the serious mind,
it's a past in which one constant is some form of pestilence.
   At present all
I can think of is the burial mound
once known as Plaguey Hill

that dominates Friar's Bush graveyard in Belfast.
The yellow of that bin is more the yellow of bog asphodel
than the yellow of forsythia or furze.

In New York City they've worked hand over fist
to set up a system of field hospitals.
Now there's been a "flattening" of the death toll from the
   novel coronavirus.

ACKNOWLEDGMENTS

Acknowledgments are due to the editors of the following, in which versions of several of these poems first appeared:

The American Poetry Review, *The Culture Cafe* (BBC Radio Ulster), *Elevations* (SiriusXM), *The Guardian*, *The Honest Ulsterman*, *Liberties*, *Little Star*, *London Review of Books*, *The New York Review of Books*, *The New Yorker*, *One Hand Clapping*, *Ploughshares*, *PN Review*, *Poetry Jukebox*, *Poetry Please* (BBC Radio 4), *Smartish Pace*, *Subtropics*, *The Times Literary Supplement*, and *The Yale Review*.

A number of these poems were included in *Binge*, a Lifeboat Poetry Pamphlet published in 2019. "Binge" is itself derived from articles published in the *Times* of London over the course of the week of May 12 through 17, 2019. Other poems were included in *The Bannisters*, a chapbook published by Vallum in 2020. "Wagtail" was published as a broadside by the King Library Press of the University of Kentucky. "Clegs and Midges" was included in *Buzz Words: Poems About Insects*, edited by Kimiko Hahn and Harold Schechter and published by Everyman's Library. "The Pangolin, or Vasty" was published as a tribute to Paul Simon by the Poetry Society of America. "The Ice Fishers" was included in *The Worked Object: Poems to the Memory of Roy Fisher*, edited by Peter Robinson and published by the University of Sheffield.

CPSIA information can be obtained
at www.ICGtesting.com
Printed in the USA
LVHW101135021122
732193LV00004B/263